Low Fat

Everyday Cookbook

STAR
FIRE

This is a Star Fire book
First published in 2006

06 08 10 09 07

1 3 5 7 9 10 8 6 4 2

Star Fire is part of
The Foundry Creative Media Company Limited
Crabtree Hall, Crabtree Lane, Fulham, London, SW6 6TY

Visit our website: www.star-fire.co.uk

ISBN-10: 1-84451-308-4 ISBN-13: 978-1-84451-308-6

Special Edition: ISBN-10: 1-84451-570-2 ISBN-13: 978-1-84451-570-7

The CIP record for this book is available from the British Library.

Printed in China

ACKNOWLEDGEMENTS

Publisher and Creative Director: Nick Wells
Project Editor and Editorial: Sarah Goulding
Design and Production: Chris Herbert, Mike Spender, Colin Rudderham and Claire Walker

Authors: Catherine Atkinson, Juliet Barker, Gina Steer, Vicki Smallwood,
Carol Tennant, Mari Mererid Williams, Elizabeth Wolf-Cohen and Simone Wright
Editorial: Gina Steer and Karen Fitzpatrick
Photography: Colin Bowling, Paul Forrester and Stephen Brayne
Home Economists and Stylists: Jacqueline Bellefontaine,
Mandy Phipps, Vicki Smallwood and Penny Stephens

All props supplied by Barbara Stewart at Surfaces

NOTE
Recipes using uncooked eggs should be avoided by infants,
the elderly, pregnant women and anyone suffering from an illness.

Contents

Soups & Starters

Fish

Poultry

Vegetarian

Vegetables & Salads

Desserts

Hygiene in the Kitchen

It is important to remember that many foods can carry some form of bacteria. In most cases, the worst it will lead to is a bout of food poisoning or gastroenteritis, although for certain people this can be serious. The risk can be reduced or eliminated, however, by good hygiene and proper cooking.

Do not buy food that is past its sell-by date and do not consume food that is past its use-by date. When buying food, use the eyes and nose. If the food looks tired, limp or a bad colour or it has a rank, acrid or simply bad smell, do not buy or eat it under any circumstances.

Take special care when preparing raw meat and fish. A separate chopping board should be used for each, and the knife, board and your hands should be thoroughly washed before handling or preparing any other food.

Regularly clean, defrost and clear out the refrigerator or freezer – it is worth checking the packaging to see exactly how long each product is safe to freeze. Avoid handling food if suffering from an upset stomach as bacteria can be passed on through food preparation.

Dish cloths and tea towels must be washed and changed regularly. Ideally use disposable cloths which should be replaced on a daily basis. More durable cloths should be left to soak in bleach, then washed in the washing machine at a high temperature.

Keep your hands, cooking utensils and food preparation surfaces clean and do not allow pets to climb on to any work surfaces.

Buying

Avoid bulk buying where possible, especially fresh produce such as meat, poultry, fish, fruit and vegetables. Fresh foods lose their nutritional value rapidly, so buying a little at a time minimises loss of nutrients. It also means your fridge won't be so full, which reduces the effectiveness of the refrigeration process.

When buying prepackaged goods such as cans or pots of cream and yogurts, check that the packaging is intact and not damaged or pierced at all. Cans should not be dented, pierced or rusty. Check the sell-by dates even for cans and packets of dry ingredients such as flour and rice. Store fresh foods in the refrigerator as soon as possible – not in the car or the office.

When buying frozen foods, ensure that they are not heavily iced on the outside and that the contents feel completely frozen. Ensure that the frozen foods have been stored in the cabinet at the correct storage level and the temperature is below -18°C/ -0.4°F. Pack in cool bags to transport home and place in the freezer as soon as possible after purchase.

Preparation

Make sure that all work surfaces and utensils are clean and dry. Hygiene should be given priority at all times. Separate chopping boards should be used for raw and cooked meats, fish and vegetables. Currently, a variety of good quality plastic boards come in various designs and colours. This makes differentiating easier and the plastic has the added hygienic advantage of being washable at high temperatures in the dishwasher. If using the board for fish, first wash in cold water, then in hot to prevent odour. Also remember that knives and utensils should always be thoroughly cleaned after use.

When cooking, be particularly careful to keep cooked and raw food separate to avoid any contamination. It is worth washing all fruits and vegetables regardless of whether they are going to be eaten raw or lightly cooked. This rule should apply even to prewashed herbs and salads.

Do not reheat food more than once. If using a microwave, always check that the food is piping hot all the way through – in theory, the food should reach 70°C/158°F and needs to be cooked at that temperature for at least three minutes to ensure that all bacteria are killed.

All poultry must be thoroughly thawed before using, including chicken and poussin. Remove the food to be thawed from the freezer and place in a shallow dish to contain the juices. Leave the food in the refrigerator until it is completely thawed. A 1.4 kg/3 lb whole chicken will take about 26–30 hours to thaw. To speed up the process, immerse the chicken in cold water, making sure that the water is changed regularly. When the joints can move freely and no ice crystals remain in the cavity, the bird is completely thawed.

Once thawed, remove the wrapper and pat the chicken dry. Place the chicken in a shallow dish, cover lightly and store as close to the base of the refrigerator as possible. The chicken should be cooked as soon as possible. Some foods can be cooked from

frozen including many prepacked foods such as soups, sauces, casseroles and breads. Where applicable follow the manufacturers' instructions.

Vegetables and fruits can also be cooked from frozen, but meats and fish should be thawed first. The only time food can be refrozen is when the food has been thoroughly thawed then cooked. Once the food has cooled then it can be frozen again, but it should only be stored for one month.

All poultry and game (except for duck) must be cooked thoroughly. When cooked, the juices will run clear on the thickest part of the bird – the best area to try is usually the thigh. Other meats, like minced meat and pork should be cooked right the way through. Fish should turn opaque, be firm in texture and break easily into large flakes.

When cooking leftovers, make sure they are reheated until piping hot and that any sauce or soup reaches boiling point first.

Storing, Refrigerating and Freezing

Meat, poultry, fish, seafood and dairy products should all be refrigerated. The temperature of the refrigerator should be between 1–5°C/34–41°F while the freezer temperature should not rise above -18°C/-0.4°F.

To ensure the optimum refrigerator and freezer temperature, avoid leaving the door open for long periods of time. Try not to overstock the refrigerator as this reduces the airflow inside and therefore the effectiveness in cooling the food within.

When refrigerating cooked food, allow it to cool down quickly and completely before refrigerating. Hot food will raise the temperature of the refrigerator and possibly affect or spoil other food stored in it.

Food within the refrigerator and freezer should always be covered. Raw and cooked food should be stored in separate parts of the refrigerator. Cooked food should be kept on the top shelves of the refrigerator, while raw meat, poultry and fish should be placed on bottom shelves to avoid

drips and cross-contamination. It is recommended that eggs should be refrigerated in order to maintain their freshness and shelf life.

Take care that frozen foods are not stored in the freezer for too long. Blanched vegetables can be stored for one month; beef, lamb, poultry and pork for six months and unblanched vegetables and fruits in syrup for a year. Oily fish and sausages should be stored for three months. Dairy products can last four to six months, while cakes and pastries can be kept in the freezer for three to six months.

High Risk Foods

Certain foods may carry risks to people who are considered vulnerable such as the elderly, the ill, pregnant women, babies, young infants and those suffering from a recurring illness.

It is advisable to avoid those foods listed below which belong to a higher-risk category.

There is a slight chance that some eggs carry the bacteria salmonella. Cook the eggs until both the yolk and the white are firm to eliminate this risk. Pay particular attention to dishes and products incorporating lightly cooked or raw eggs which should be eliminated from the diet. Hollandaise sauce, mayonnaise, mousses, soufflés and meringues all use raw or lightly cooked eggs, as do custard-based dishes, ice creams and sorbets. These are all considered high-risk foods to the vulnerable groups mentioned above.

Certain meats and poultry also carry the potential risk of salmonella and so should be cooked thoroughly

until the juices run clear and there is no pinkness left. Unpasteurised products such as milk, cheese (especially soft cheese), pâté, meat (both raw and cooked) all have the potential risk of listeria and should be avoided.

When buying seafood, buy from a reputable source which has a high turnover to ensure freshness. Fish should have bright clear eyes, shiny skin and bright pink or red gills. The fish should feel stiff to the touch, with a slight smell of sea air and iodine. The flesh of fish steaks and fillets should be translucent with no signs of discolouration. Molluscs such as scallops, clams and mussels are sold fresh and are still alive. Avoid any that are open or do not close when tapped lightly. In the same way, univalves such as cockles or winkles should withdraw back into their shells when lightly prodded. When choosing cephalopods such as squid and octopus they should have a firm flesh and pleasant sea smell.

As with all fish, whether it is shellfish or seafish, care is required when freezing it. It is imperative to check whether the fish has been frozen before. If it has been frozen, then it should not be frozen again under any circumstances.

Nutrition The Role of Essential Nutrients

A healthy and well-balanced diet is the body's primary energy source. In children, it constitutes the building blocks for future health as well as providing lots of energy. In adults, it encourages self-healing and regeneration within the body. A well-balanced diet will provide the body with all the essential nutrients it needs. This can be achieved by eating a variety of foods, demonstrated in the pyramid below.

FATS

PROTEINS

milk,   meat, fish,
yogurt   poultry, eggs,
and cheese   nuts and pulses

FRUITS AND VEGETABLES

STARCHY CARBOHYDRATES

cereals, potatoes, bread, rice and pasta

FATS

Fats fall into two categories: saturated and unsaturated. It is very important that a healthy balance is achieved within the diet. Fats are an essential part of the diet: they are a source of energy and provide essential fatty acids and fat soluble vitamins. The right balance of fats should boost the body's immunity to infection and keep muscles, nerves and arteries in good condition. Saturated fats are of animal origin and are hard when stored at room temperature. They can be found in dairy produce, meat, eggs, margarines and hard white cooking fat (lard) as well as in manufactured products such as pies, biscuits and cakes. A high intake of saturated fat over many years has been proven to increase heart disease and high blood cholesterol levels and often leads to weight gain. The aim of a healthy diet is to keep the fat content low in the foods that we eat. Lowering the amount of saturated fat that we consume is very important, but this does not mean that it is good to consume lots of other types of fat.

There are two kinds of unsaturated fats: polyunsaturated and monounsaturated. Polyunsaturated fats include safflower, soybean, corn and sesame oils. Within the polyunsaturated group are Omega oils. The Omega-3 oils are of significant interest because they have been found to be particularly beneficial to coronary health and can encourage brain growth and development. Omega-3 oils are derived from oily fish such as salmon, mackerel, herring, pilchards and sardines. It is recommended that we should eat these types of fish at least once a week. However, for those who do not eat fish or who are vegetarians, liver oil supplements are available in most supermarkets and health shops. It is suggested that these supplements should be taken on a daily basis. The most popular oils that are high in monounsaturates are olive oil, sunflower oil and peanut oil. The Mediterranean diet which is based on a diet high in monounsaturated fats is recommended for heart health. Monounsaturated fats are also known to help reduce the levels of cholesterol.

PROTEINS

Composed of amino acids – proteins' building blocks – proteins perform a wide variety of essential functions for the body, including supplying energy and building and repairing tissues. Good sources of proteins are eggs, milk, yogurt, cheese, meat, fish, poultry, eggs, nuts and pulses. (See the second level of the pyramid.) Some of these foods, however, contain saturated fats. To strike a nutritional balance, eat generous amounts of vegetable protein foods such as soya, beans, lentils, peas and nuts.

FRUITS AND VEGETABLES

Not only are fruits and vegetables the most visually appealing foods, but they are extremely good for us, providing essential vitamins and minerals essential for growth, repair and protection in the human body. Fruits and vegetables are low in calories and are responsible for regulating the body's metabolic processes and controlling the composition of its fluids and cells.

MINERALS

CALCIUM Important for healthy bones and teeth, nerve transmission, muscle contraction, blood clotting and hormone function. Calcium promotes a healthy heart, improves skin, relieves aching muscles and bones, maintains the correct acid-alkaline balance and reduces menstrual cramps. Good sources are dairy products, the bones of small fish, nuts, pulses, fortified white flours, breads and green leafy vegetables.

CHROMIUM Part of the glucose tolerance factor, chromium balances blood sugar levels, helps to normalise hunger and reduce cravings, improves lifespan, helps protect DNA and is essential for heart function. Good sources are brewer's yeast, wholemeal bread, rye bread, oysters, potatoes, green peppers, butter and parsnips.

IODINE Important for the manufacture of thyroid hormones and for normal development. Good sources of iodine are seafood, seaweed, milk and dairy products.

IRON As a component of haemoglobin, iron carries oxygen around the body. It is vital for normal growth and development. Good sources are liver, corned beef, red meat, fortified breakfast cereals, pulses, green leafy vegetables, egg yolk, cocoa and cocoa products.

MAGNESIUM Important for efficient functioning of metabolic enzymes and development of the skeleton. Magnesium promotes healthy muscles by helping them to relax and is therefore good for PMS. It is also important for heart muscles and the nervous system. Good sources are nuts, green vegetables, meat, cereals, milk and yogurt.

PHOSPHORUS Forms and maintains bones and teeth, builds muscle tissue, helps maintain pH of the body and aids metabolism and energy production. Phosphorus is present in almost all foods.

POTASSIUM Enables nutrients to move into cells while waste products move out; promotes healthy nerves and muscles; maintains fluid balance in the body; helps secretion of insulin for blood sugar control to produce constant energy; relaxes muscles; maintains heart functioning and stimulates gut movement to encourage proper elimination. Good sources are fruit, vegetables, milk and bread.

SELENIUM Antioxidant properties help to protect against free radicals and carcinogens. Selenium reduces inflammation, stimulates the immune system to fight infections, promotes a healthy heart and helps vitamin E's action. It is also required for the male reproductive system and is needed for metabolism. Good sources are tuna, liver, kidney, meat, eggs, cereals, nuts and dairy products.

SODIUM Important in helping to control body fluid and balance, preventing dehydration. Sodium is involved in muscle and nerve function and helps move nutrients into cells. All foods are good sources. Processed, pickled and salted foods are richest in sodium but should be eaten in moderation.

ZINC Important for metabolism and the healing of wounds. It also aids ability to cope with stress, promotes a healthy nervous system and brain especially in the growing foetus, aids bone and teeth formation and is essential for constant energy. Good sources are liver, meat, pulses, whole-grain cereals, nuts and oysters.

VITAMINS

VITAMIN A Important for cell growth and development and for the formation of visual pigments in the eye. Vitamin A comes in two forms: retinol and beta-carotenes. Retinol is found in liver, meat and meat products and whole milk and its products. Beta-carotene is a powerful antioxidant and is found in red and yellow fruits and vegetables such as carrots, mangoes and apricots.

VITAMIN B1 Important in releasing energy from carbohydrate-containing foods. Good sources are yeast and yeast products, bread, fortified breakfast cereals and potatoes.

VITAMIN B2 Important for metabolism of proteins, fats and carbohydrates to produce energy. Good sources are meat, yeast extracts, fortified breakfast cereals and milk and its products.

VITAMIN B3 Required for the metabolism of food into energy production. Good sources are milk and milk products, fortified breakfast cereals, pulses, meat, poultry and eggs.

VITAMIN B5 Important for the metabolism of food and energy production. All foods are good sources but especially fortified breakfast cereals, whole-grain bread and dairy products.

VITAMIN B6 Important for metabolism of protein and fat. Vitamin B6 may also be involved in the regulation of sex hormones. Good sources are liver, fish, pork, soya beans and peanuts.

VITAMIN B12 Important for the production of red blood cells and DNA. It is vital for growth and the nervous system. Good sources are meat, fish, eggs, poultry and milk.

BIOTIN Important for metabolism of fatty acids. Good sources of biotin are liver, kidney, eggs and nuts. Micro-organisms also manufacture this vitamin in the gut.

VITAMIN C Important for healing wounds and the formation of collagen which keeps skin and bones strong. It is an important antioxidant. Good sources are fruits, especially soft summer fruits, and vegetables.

VITAMIN D Important for absorption and handling of calcium to help build bone strength. Good sources are oily fish, eggs, whole milk and milk products, margarine and of course sufficient exposure to sunlight, as vitamin D is made in the skin.

VITAMIN E Important as an antioxidant vitamin helping to protect cell membranes from damage. Good sources are vegetable oils, margarines, seeds, nuts and green vegetables.

FOLIC ACID Critical during pregnancy for the development of the brain and nerves. It is always essential for brain and nerve function and is needed for utilising protein and red blood cell formation. Good sources are whole-grain cereals, fortified breakfast cereals, green leafy vegetables, oranges and liver.

VITAMIN K Important for controlling blood clotting. Good sources are cauliflower, Brussels sprouts, lettuce, cabbage, beans, broccoli, peas, asparagus, potatoes, corn oil, tomatoes and milk.

CARBOHYDRATES

Carbohydrates are an energy source and come in two forms: starch and sugar. Starch carbohydrates are also known as complex carbohydrates and they include all cereals, potatoes, breads, rice and pasta. (See the fourth level of the pyramid). Eating whole-grain varieties of these foods also provides fibre. Diets high in fibre are believed to be beneficial in helping to prevent bowel cancer and can also keep cholesterol down. High-fibre diets are also good for those concerned about weight gain. Fibre is bulky and fills the stomach, therefore reducing hunger pangs. Sugar carbohydrates which are also known as fast release carbohydrates because of the quick fix of energy they give to the body, and include sugar and sugar-sweetened products such as jams and syrups. Milk provides lactose which is a milk sugar and fruits provide fructose which is a fruit sugar.

Guidelines for Different Age Groups

Good food plays such an important role in everyone's life. From infancy through to adulthood, a healthy diet provides the body's foundation and building blocks and teaches children healthy eating habits. Studies have shown that these eating habits stay with us into later life helping us to maintain a healthier lifestyle as adults. This reduces the risk of illness, disease and certain medical problems.

Striking a healthy balance is important and at certain stages in life, this balance may need to be adjusted to help our bodies cope.

As babies and children, during pregnancy and in later life, our diet assists us in achieving optimal health. So how do we go about achieving this?

We know that certain foods, such as oily fish, for example, are advantageous to all – they are rich in Omega-3 fatty acids which have been linked with more efficient brain functioning and better memory. They can also help lower the risk of cancer and heart disease. But are there any other steps we can take to maximise health benefits through our diet?

Babies & Young Children

Babies should not be given solids until they are at least six months old, from which point new tastes and textures can be introduced to their diets. Probably the easiest and cheapest way is to adapt the food that the rest of the family eat. Babies under the age of one should be given breast milk or formula. From the age of one to two, whole milk should be given and from two to five semi-skimmed milk can be given. From then on, skimmed milk can be introduced if desired.

The first foods for babies under six months should be of a purée-like consistency, which is smooth and fairly liquid, therefore making it easy to swallow. This can be done using an electric blender or hand blender or just by pushing food through a sieve to remove any lumps. Remember, however, that babies still need high levels of milk.

Babies over six months old should still be having puréed food, but the consistency of their diet can be made progressively lumpier. Around the 10 month mark, most babies are able to manage food cut up into small pieces.

So, what food groups do babies and small children need? Like adults, a high proportion of their diet should contain grains such as cereal, pasta, bread and rice. Be careful, however, as babies and small children cannot cope with too much high-fibre food in their diet.

Fresh fruits and vegetables should be introduced, as well as a balance of dairy and meat proteins and only a small proportion of fats and sweets. Research points out that delaying the introduction of foods which could cause allergies during the first year (such as cow's milk, wheat, eggs, cheese, yogurt and nuts) can significantly reduce the risk of certain food allergies later on in life. (NB: Peanuts should never be given to children under five years old.)

Seek a doctor or health visitor's advice regarding babies and toddlers. Limit sugar in young children's diets as it provides only empty calories. Use less processed sugars (muscovado is very sweet, so the amount used can be reduced) or incorporate less refined alternatives such as dried fruits, dates, rice syrup or honey. (NB: Honey should not be given to infants under one year of age.)

As in a low-fat diet, it is best to eliminate fried foods and avoid adding salt – especially for under one-year-olds and young infants. Instead, introduce herbs and gentle spices to make food appetising. The more varied the tastes that children experience in their formative years, the wider the range of foods they will accept later in life.

Pregnancy

During pregnancy, women are advised to take extra vitamin and mineral supplements. Pregnant women benefit from a healthy balanced diet, rich in fresh fruit and vegetables, and full of essential vitamins and minerals. Oily fish, such as salmon, not only give the body essential fats but also provide high levels of bio-available calcium.

Certain food groups, however, hold risks during pregnancy. This section gives advice on everyday foods and those that should be avoided.

Cheese

Pregnant women should avoid all soft mould-ripened cheese such as brie. Also, if pregnant, do not eat cheese such as parmesan or blue-veined cheese like stilton as they carry the risk of potential listeria. It is fine for pregnant women to carry on eating hard cheese like cheddar, as well as cottage cheese.

Eggs

There is a slight chance that some eggs will carry salmonella. Cooking the eggs until both the yolk and white are firm will eliminate this risk. However, particular attention should be paid to dishes and products that incorporate lightly cooked or raw eggs, homemade mayonnaise or similar sauces, mousses, soufflés, meringues, ice cream and sorbets. Commercially produced products, such as mayonnaise, are made with pasteurised eggs and may be eaten safely. If in doubt, play safe and avoid it.

Ready-made meals and ready-to-eat items

Previously cooked, then chilled meals are now widely available, but those from the chilled counter can contain bacteria. Avoid prepacked salads in dressings and other foods which are sold loose from chilled cabinets. Also do not eat raw or partly cooked meats, pâté, unpasteurised milk and soil-dirty fruits and vegetables as they can cause toxoplasmosis.

Meat and fish

Certain meats and poultry carry the potential risk of salmonella and should be cooked thoroughly until the juices run clear and there is no pinkness left.

Pay particular attention when buying and cooking fish (especially shellfish). Buy only the freshest fish which should smell salty but not strong or fishy.

Look for bright eyes and reject any with sunken eyes. The bodies should look fresh, plump and shiny. Avoid any fish with dry, shrivelled or damp bodies.

It is also best to avoid any shellfish while pregnant unless it is definitely fresh and thoroughly cooked. Shellfish also contains harmful bacteria and viruses.

Later Life

So what about later on in life? As the body gets older, we can help stave off infection and illness through our diet. There is evidence to show that the immune system becomes weaker as we get older, which can increase the risk of suffering from cancer and other illnesses. Maintaining a diet rich in antioxidants, fresh fruits and vegetables, plant oils and oily fish is especially beneficial in order to either prevent these illnesses or minimise their effects. As with all age groups, the body benefits from the five-a-day eating plan – try to eat five portions of fruit or vegetables each day. Leafy green vegetables, in particular, are rich in antioxidants. Cabbage, broccoli, Brussels sprouts, cauliflower and kale contain particularly high levels of antioxidants, which lower the risk of cancer.

Foods which are green in colour tend to provide nutrients essential for healthy nerves, muscles andhormones, while foods red in colour protect against cardiovascular disease. Other foods that can also assist in preventing cardiovascular disease and ensuring a healthy heart include vitamins E and C, oily fish and essential fats (such as extra virgin olive oil). They help lower blood cholesterol levels and clear arteries. A diet high in fresh fruits and vegetables and low in salt and saturated fats can considerably reduce heart disease.

Other foods have recognised properties. Certain types of mushrooms are known to boost the immune system, while garlic not only boosts the immune system but also protects the body against cancer. Live yogurt, too, has healthy properties as it contains gut-friendly bacteria which help digestion.

Some foods can help to balance the body's hormone levels during the menopause. For example, soya regulates hormone levels. Studies have shown that a regular intake of soya can help to protect the body against breast and prostate cancer.

A balanced, healthy diet, rich in fresh fruits and vegetables, carbohydrates, proteins and essential fats and low in saturates, can help the body protect itself throughout its life. It really is worth spending a little extra time and effort when shopping or even just thinking about what to cook.

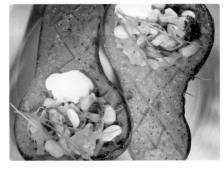

Store Cupboard Essentials
Low–fat Ingredients for a Healthy Lifestyle

Low-fat cooking has often been associated with the stigma that reducing fat reduces flavour. This simply is not the case, which is great news for those choosing a lower-fat diet. Modern lifestyles are naturally shifting towards lower-fat and cholesterol diets so there is no need to compromise on the choice of foods we eat thanks to the increasing number of lower-fat products now available in the high street.

The store cupboard is a good place to start when cooking low-fat meals. Most of us have fairly limited cooking and preparation time available during the week, so choose to experiment during weekends. When time is of the essence, or friends arrive unannounced, it is always a good idea, especially when following a low-fat diet, to have some well thought out basics in the cupboard, that is foods that are high on flavour and low in fat.

As store cupboard ingredients keep reasonably well, it really is worth making a trip to a good speciality grocery shop. Our society's growing obsession in recent years with travel and food from around the world has led us to seek out alternative ingredients with which to experiment and incorporate into our cooking. Consequently, supermarket chains have had to broaden their product range and often have a specialist range of imported ingredients from around the world.

If the grocers or local supermarket only carries a limited choice of products, do not despair. The Internet now offers freedom to the food shopaholics amongst us. There are some fantastic food sites (both local and international) where food can be purchased and delivery arranged online.

When thinking about essentials, think of flavour, something that is going to add to a dish without increasing its fat content. It is worth spending a little bit more money on these products to make flavoursome dishes that will help stop the urge to snack on fatty foods.

Store Cupboard Hints

There are many different types of store cupboard ingredients readily available – including myriad varieties of rice and pasta – which can provide much of the carbohydrate required in our daily diets. Store the ingredients in a cool dark place and remember to rotate the store cupboard ingredients. The ingredients will be safe to use for six months.

Bulghur wheat A cracked wheat which is often used in tabbouleh. Bulghur wheat is a good source of complex carbohydrate.

Couscous Now available in instant form, couscous just needs to be covered with boiling water then forked. Couscous is a precooked wheat semolina. Traditional couscous needs to be steamed and is available from health food stores. This type of couscous contains more nutrients than the instant variety.

Dried fruit The ready-to-eat variety are particularly good as they are plump, juicy and do not need to be soaked. They are fantastic when puréed into a compote, added to water and heated to make a pie filling and when added to stuffing mixtures. They are also good cooked with meats, rice or couscous.

Flours A useful addition (particularly cornflour) which can be used to thicken sauces. It is worth mentioning that whole-grain flour should not be stored for too long at room temperature as the fats may turn rancid. While not strictly a flour, cornmeal is a very versatile low-fat ingredient, which can be used when making dumplings and gnocchi.

Noodles Noodles are also very useful and can accompany any far-eastern dish. They are low-fat and also available in the wholewheat variety. Rice noodles are available for those who have gluten-free diets and, like pasta noodles, provide slow-release energy to the body.

Pasta It is good to have a mixture of wholewheat and plain pasta as well as a wide variety of flavoured pastas. Whether fresh (it can also be frozen) or dried, pasta is a versatile ingredient with which to provide the body with slow-release energy. It comes in many different sizes and shapes; from the tiny tubettini (which can be added to soups to create a more substantial dish), to penne, fusilli, rigatoni and conchiglie, up to the larger cannelloni and lasagne sheets.

Pot and pearl barley Pot barley is the compelte barley grain whereas pearl barley has the outer husk removed. A high cereal diet can help to prevent bowel disorders and diseases.

Pulses A vital ingredient for the store cupboard, they are easy to store, have a very high nutritional value and are great when added to soups, casseroles, curries and hot pots. Pulses also act as a thickener, whether flavoured or on their own. They come in two forms; either dried (in which case they generally need to be soaked overnight and then cooked before use – it is important to follow the instructions on the back of the packet), or canned, which is a convenient timesaver because the preparation of dried pulses can take a while. If buying canned pulses try to buy the variety in water with no added salt or sugar. These simply need to be drained and rinsed before being added to a dish.

Kidney beans, borlotti, cannellini, butter, flageolet beans, split peas and lentils, all make tasty additions to any dish. Baked beans are a favourite with everyone and many shops now stock the organic variety, which have no added salt or sugar but are sweetened with fruit juice instead.

When boiling previously dried pulses, remember that salt should not be added as this will make the skins tough and inedible. Puy lentils are a smaller variety. They often have mottled skins and are particularly good for cooking in slow dishes as they hold their shape and firm texture particularly well.

Rice Basmati and Thai fragrant rice are well suited to Thai and Indian curries as the fine grains absorb the sauce and their delicate creaminess balances the

pungency of the spices. Arborio is only one type of risotto rice. Many are available depending on whether the risotto is meant to accompany meat, fish or vegetable dishes. When cooked, rice swells to create a substantial low-fat dish. Easy-cook American rice, both plain and whole-grain, is great for casseroles and for stuffing meat, fish and vegetables as it holds its shape and firmness. Pudding rice can be used in a variety of ways to create an irresistible dessert.

Stock Good-quality stock is a must in low-fat cooking as it provides a good flavour base for many dishes. Many supermarkets now carry a variety of fresh and organic stocks which although need refrigeration, are probably one of the most time- and effort-saving ingredients available. There is also a fairly large range of dried stock, perhaps the best being bouillon, a high-quality form of stock (available in powder or liquid form) which can be added to any dish whether it be a sauce, casserole, pie or soup.

Many people favour meals which can be prepared and cooked in 30–45 minutes, so helpful ingredients which kick-start a sauce are great. A good-quality passata sauce or canned plum tomatoes can act as the foundation for any sauce, as can a good-quality green or red pesto. Other handy store cupboard additions include tapenade, mustard and anchovies. These ingredients have very distinctive tastes and are particularly flavoursome. Roasted red pepper sauce and sundried tomato purée, which tends to be sweeter and more intensely flavoured than regular tomato purée are also very useful.

Vinegar is another worthwhile store cupboard essential and with so many uses it is worth splashing out on a really good-quality balsamic and wine vinegar. Herbs and spices are a must, so it is worth taking a look at the section on pages 14–15. Using herbs when cooking at home should reduce the temptation to buy ready-made sauces. Often these types of sauces contain large amounts of sugar and additives.

Yeast extract is also a good store cupboard ingredient, which can pep up sauces, soups and casseroles and adds a little substance particularly to vegetarian dishes.

Eastern flavours offer a lot of scope where low-fat cooking is concerned. Flavourings such as fish sauce, soy sauce, red and green curry paste and Chinese rice wine all offer mouthwatering low-fat flavours to any dish.

For those who are incredibly short on time, or who rarely shop, it is now possible to purchase a selection of readily prepared freshly minced garlic, ginger and chilli (available in jars which can be kept in the refrigerator).

As well as these store cupboard additions, many shops and especially supermarkets provide a wide choice of products and carry a wide range of low-fat products. Where possible, invest in the leanest cut of meat and substitute saturated fats such as cream, butter and cheese with low-fat or half-fat alternatives, such as half-fat crème fraîche, fromage frais, butter and cheese.

Herbs and Spices

Herbs are easy to grow and a garden is not needed as they can easily thrive on a small patio, window box or even on a windowsill. It is worth the effort to plant a few herbs as they do not require much attention or nurturing. The reward will be a range of fresh herbs available whenever needed, and fresh flavours that cannot be beaten to add to any dish that is being prepared.

While fresh herbs should be picked or bought as close as possible to the time of use, freeze-dried and dried herbs and spices will usually keep for around six months.

The best idea is to buy little and often, and to store the herbs in airtight jars in a cool dark cupboard. Fresh herbs tend to have a milder flavour than dried and equate to around one level tablespoon of fresh to one level teaspoon of dried. As a result, quantities used in cooking should be altered accordingly. A variety of herbs and spices and their uses are listed below.

ALLSPICE
The dark allspice berries come whole or ground and have a flavour similar to that of cinnamon, cloves and nutmeg. Although not the same as mixed spices, allspice can be used with pickles, relishes, cakes and milk puddings or whole in meat and fish dishes.

ANISEED
Aniseed comes in whole seeds or ground. It has a strong aroma and flavour and should be used sparingly in baking and salad dressings.

BASIL
Best fresh but also available in dried form, basil can be used raw or cooked. It works well in many dishes but is particularly well suited to tomato-based dishes and sauces, salads and Mediterranean recipes.

BAY LEAVES
Bay leaves are available in fresh or dried form as well as ground. They make up part of a bouquet garni and are particularly delicious when added to meat and poultry dishes, soups, stews, vegetable dishes and stuffing. They also impart a spicy flavour to milk puddings and egg custards.

BOUQUET GARNI
Bouquet garni is a bouquet of fresh herbs tied with a piece of string or in a small piece of muslin. It is used to flavour casseroles, stews and stocks or sauces. The herbs that are normally used are parsley, thyme, and bay leaves.

CARAWAY SEEDS
Caraway seeds have a warm sweet taste and are often used in breads and cakes but are delicious with cabbage dishes and pickles as well.

CAYENNE
Cayenne is the powdered form of a red chilli pepper said to be native to Cayenne. It is similar in appearance to paprika and can be used sparingly to add a fiery kick to many dishes.

CARDAMOM
Cardamom has a distinctive sweet, rich taste and can be bought whole in the pod, in seed form or ground. This sweet aromatic spice is delicious in curries, rice, cakes and biscuits and is great served with rice pudding and fruit.

CHERVIL
Reminiscent of parsley and available either in fresh or dried form, chervil has a faintly sweet, spicy flavour and is particularly good in soups, cheese dishes, stews and with eggs.

CHILLI
Available whole, fresh, dried and in powdered form, red chillies tend to be sweeter in taste than their green counterparts. They are particularly associated with Spanish and Mexican-style cooking and curries, but are also delicious with pickles, dips, sauces and in pizza toppings.

CHIVES
Best used when fresh but also available in dried form, this member of the onion family is ideal for use when a delicate onion flavour is required. Chives are good with eggs, cheese, fish and vegetable dishes. They also work well as a garnish for soups, meat and vegetable dishes.

CINNAMON
Cinnamon comes in the form of reddish-brown sticks of bark from an evergreen tree and has a sweet, pungent aroma. Either whole or ground, cinnamon is delicious in cakes and milk puddings, particularly with apple, and is used in mulled wine and for preserving.

CLOVES
Mainly used whole although also available ground, cloves have a very warm, sweet pungent aroma and can be used to stud roast ham and pork, in mulled wine and punch and when pickling fruit. When ground, they can be used in making mincemeat and in Christmas puddings and biscuits.

CORIANDER
Coriander seeds have an orangey flavour and are available whole or ground. Coriander is particularly delicious (whether whole or roughly ground) in casseroles, curries and as a pickling spice. The leaves are used to flavour spicy aromatic dishes as well as a garnish.

CUMIN
Also available ground or as whole seeds, cumin has a strong, slightly bitter flavour. It is one of the main ingredients in curry powder and compliments many fish, meat and rice dishes.

DILL
Dill leaves are available fresh or dried and have a mild flavour, while the seeds are slightly bitter. Dill is particularly good with salmon, new potatoes and in sauces. The seeds are good in pickles and vegetable dishes.

FENNEL
Whole seeds or ground, fennel has a fragrant, sweet aniseed flavour and is sometimes known as the fish herb because it compliments fish dishes so well.

GINGER
Ginger comes in many forms but primarily as a fresh root and in dried ground form, which can be used in baking, curries, pickles, sauces and Chinese cooking.

LEMON GRASS
Available fresh and dried, with a subtle, aromatic, lemony flavour, lemon grass is essential to Thai cooking. It is also delicious when added to soups, poultry and fish dishes.

MACE
The outer husk of nutmeg has a milder nutmeg flavour and can be used in pickles, cheese dishes, stewed fruits, sauces and hot punch.

MARJORAM
Often dried, marjoram has a sweet slightly spicy flavour, which tastes fantastic when added to stuffing, meat or tomato-based dishes.

MINT
Available fresh or dried, mint has a strong, sweet aroma which is delicious in a sauce or jelly to serve with lamb. It is also great with fresh peas and new potatoes and is an essential ingredient in Pimms.

MUSTARD SEED
These yellow and brown seeds are available whole or ground and are often found in pickles, relishes, cheese dishes, dressings, curries and as an accompaniment to meat.

NUTMEG
The large whole seeds have a warm, sweet taste and compliment custards, milk puddings, cheese dishes, parsnips and creamy soups.

OREGANO
The strongly flavoured dried leaves of oregano are similar to marjoram and are used extensively in Italian and Greek cooking.

PAPRIKA
Paprika often comes in two varieties. One is quite sweet and mild and the other has a slight bite to it. Paprika is made from the fruit of the sweet pepper and is good in meat and poultry dishes as well as a garnish. The rule of buying herbs and spices little and often applies particularly to paprika as unfortunately it does not keep particularly well.

PARSLEY
The stems as well as the leaves of parsley can be used to compliment most savoury dishes as they contain the most flavour. They can also be used as a garnish.

PEPPER
This comes in white and black peppercorns and is best freshly ground. Both add flavour to most dishes, sauces and gravies. Black pepper has a more robust flavour, while white pepper is much more delicate.

POPPY SEEDS
These tiny, grey-black coloured seeds impart a sweet, nutty flavour when added to biscuits, vegetable dishes, dressings and cheese dishes.

ROSEMARY
Delicious fresh or dried, these small, needle-like leaves have a sweet aroma which is particularly good with lamb, stuffing and vegetable dishes. Also delicious when added to charcoal on the barbecue to give a piquant flavour to meat and corn on the cob.

SAFFRON
Deep orange in colour, saffron is traditionally used in paella, rice and cakes but is also delicious with poultry. Saffron is the most expensive of all spices.

SAGE
Fresh or dried sage leaves have a pungent, slightly bitter taste which is delicious with pork and poultry, sausages, stuffing and with stuffed pasta when tossed in a little butter and fresh sage.

SAVORY
This herb resembles thyme, but has a softer flavour that particularly compliments all types of fish and beans.

SESAME
Sesame seeds have a nutty taste, especially when toasted, and are delicious in baking, on salads, or with far-Eastern cooking.

TARRAGON
The fresh or dried leaves of tarragon have a sweet aromatic taste which is particularly good with poultry, seafood, fish, creamy sauces and stuffing.

THYME
Available fresh or dried, thyme has a pungent flavour and is included in bouquet garni. It compliments many meat and poultry dishes and stuffing.

TURMERIC
Turmeric is obtained from the root of a lily from southeast Asia. This root is ground and has a brilliant yellow colour. It has a bitter, peppery flavour and is often combined for use in curry powder and mustard. Also delicious in pickles, relishes and dressings.

Mushroom & Sherry Soup

INGREDIENTS

Serves 4

4 slices day old white bread

zest of ½ lemon

1 tbsp lemon juice

salt and freshly ground black pepper

125 g/4 oz assorted wild mushrooms,
   lightly rinsed

125 g/4 oz baby button
   mushrooms, wiped

2 tsp olive oil

1 garlic clove, peeled and crushed

6 spring onions, trimmed and
   diagonally sliced

600 ml/1 pint chicken stock

4 tbsp dry sherry

1 tbsp freshly snipped chives,
   to garnish

HELPFUL HINT

To achieve very fine shreds, use a zester, obtainable from all cook shops. Or thinly peel the fruit with a vegetable peeler, then shred with a small sharp knife. When grating fruit, use a clean, dry pastry brush to remove the rind from the grater.

1   Preheat the oven to 180°C/ 350°F/Gas Mark 4. Remove the crusts from the bread and cut the bread into small cubes.

2   In a large bowl toss the cubes of bread with the lemon rind and juice, 2 tablespoons of water and plenty of freshly ground black pepper.

3   Spread the bread cubes on to a lightly oiled, large baking tray and bake for 20 minutes until golden and crisp.

4   If the wild mushrooms are small, leave some whole. Otherwise, thinly slice all the mushrooms and reserve.

5   Heat the oil in a saucepan. Add the garlic and spring onions and cook for 1–2 minutes.

6   Add the mushrooms and cook for 3–4 minutes until they start to soften. Add the chicken stock and stir to mix.

7   Bring to the boil, then reduce the heat to a gentle simmer. Cover and cook for 10 minutes.

8   Stir in the sherry, and season to taste with a little salt and pepper. Pour into warmed bowls, sprinkle over the chives, and serve immediately with the lemon croûtons.

2

4

6

Chinese Chicken Soup

INGREDIENTS

Serves 4

225 g/8 oz cooked chicken
1 tsp oil
6 spring onions, trimmed and
   diagonally sliced
1 red chilli, deseeded and
   finely chopped
1 garlic clove, peeled
   and crushed
2.5 cm/1 inch piece root ginger,
   peeled and finely grated
1 litre/1³/₄ pint chicken stock
150 g/5 oz medium egg noodles
1 carrot, peeled and cut
   into matchsticks
125 g/4 oz beansprouts
2 tbsp soy sauce
1 tbsp fish sauce
fresh coriander leaves,
   to garnish

1 Remove any skin from the chicken. Place on a chopping board and use two forks to tear the chicken into fine shreds.

2 Heat the oil in a large saucepan and fry the spring onions and chilli for 1 minute.

3 Add the garlic and ginger and cook for another minute.

4 Stir in the chicken stock and gradually bring the mixture to the boil.

5 Break up the noodles a little and add to the boiling stock with the carrot.

6 Stir to mix, then reduce the heat to a simmer and cook for 3–4 minutes.

7 Add the shredded chicken, beansprouts, soy sauce and fish sauce and stir.

8 Cook for a further 2–3 minutes until piping hot. Ladle the soup into bowls and sprinkle with the coriander leaves. Serve immediately.

1

5

7

Carrot & Ginger Soup

INGREDIENTS

Serves 4

4 slices of bread, crusts removed
1 tsp yeast extract
2 tsp olive oil
1 onion, peeled and chopped
1 garlic clove, peeled and crushed
½ tsp ground ginger
450 g/1 lb carrots, peeled
  and chopped
1 litre/1¾ pint vegetable stock
2.5 cm/1 inch piece of root ginger,
  peeled and finely grated
salt and freshly ground black pepper
1 tbsp lemon juice

To garnish:
chives
lemon zest

TASTY TIP

Serve with slices of bruschetta, made by lightly grilling thick slices of ciabatta bread on both sides. While still warm rub the top of the bruschetta with a whole, peeled clove of garlic and drizzle with a little good quality extra-virgin olive oil.

1 Preheat the oven to 180°C/ 350°F/Gas Mark 4. Roughly chop the bread. Dissolve the yeast extract in 2 tablespoons of warm water and mix with the bread.

2 Spread the bread cubes over a lightly oiled baking tray and bake for 20 minutes, turning half way through. Remove from the oven and reserve.

3 Heat the oil in a large saucepan. Gently cook the onion and garlic for 3–4 minutes.

4 Stir in the ground ginger and cook for 1 minute to release the flavour.

5 Add the chopped carrots, then stir in the stock and the fresh ginger. Simmer gently for 15 minutes.

6 Remove from the heat and allow to cool a little. Blend until smooth, then season to taste with salt and pepper. Stir in the lemon juice. Garnish with the chives and lemon zest and serve immediately.

2

4

6

Italian Bean Soup

INGREDIENTS

Serves 4

2 tsp olive oil

1 leek, washed and chopped

1 garlic clove, peeled
  and crushed

2 tsp dried oregano

75 g/3 oz green beans, trimmed and
  cut into bite-size pieces

410 g can cannellini beans, drained
  and rinsed

75 g/3 oz small pasta shapes

1 litre/1¾ pint vegetable stock

8 cherry tomatoes

salt and freshly ground
  black pepper

3 tbsp freshly shredded basil

1. Heat the oil in a large saucepan. Add the leek, garlic and oregano and cook gently for 5 minutes, stirring occasionally.

2. Stir in the green beans and the cannellini beans. Sprinkle in the pasta and pour in the stock.

3. Bring the stock mixture to the boil, then reduce the heat to a simmer.

4. Cook for 12–15 minutes or until the vegetables are tender and the pasta is cooked to al dente. Stir occasionally.

5. In a heavy-based frying pan, dry-fry the tomatoes over a high heat until they soften and the skins begin to blacken.

6. Gently crush the tomatoes in the pan with the back of a spoon and add to the soup.

7. Season to taste with salt and pepper. Stir in the shredded basil and serve immediately.

TASTY TIP

This soup will taste even better the day after it has been made. Make the soup the day before you intend serving it and add a little extra stock when reheating.

2

5

6

Tomato & Basil Soup

INGREDIENTS

Serves 4

1.1 kg/2½ lb ripe tomatoes,
  cut in half
2 garlic cloves
1 tsp olive oil
1 tbsp balsamic vinegar
1 tbsp dark brown sugar
1 tbsp tomato purée
300 ml/½ pint vegetable stock
6 tbsp low-fat natural yogurt
2 tbsp freshly chopped basil
salt and freshly ground black pepper
small basil leaves, to garnish

TASTY TIP

Use the sweetest type of tomatoes available as it makes a big difference to the flavour of the soup. Many supermarkets now stock speciality ranges grown slowly and matured for longer on the vine to give them an intense flavour. If these are unavailable, add a little extra sugar to bring out the flavour.

1 Preheat the oven to 200°C/ 400°F/Gas Mark 6. Evenly spread the tomatoes and unpeeled garlic in a single layer in a large roasting tin.

2 Mix the oil and vinegar together. Drizzle over the tomatoes and sprinkle with the dark brown sugar.

3 Roast the tomatoes in the preheated oven for 20 minutes until tender and lightly charred in places.

4 Remove from the oven and allow to cool slightly. When cool enough to handle, squeeze the softened flesh of the garlic from the papery skin. Place with the charred tomatoes in a nylon sieve over a saucepan.

5 Press the garlic and tomato through the sieve with the back of a wooden spoon.

6 When all the flesh has been sieved, add the tomato purée and vegetable stock to the pan. Heat gently, stirring occasionally.

7 In a small bowl beat the yogurt and basil together and season to taste with salt and pepper. Stir the basil yogurt into the soup. Garnish with basil leaves and serve immediately.

2

4

7

Prawn & Chilli Soup

INGREDIENTS

Serves 4

2 spring onions, trimmed
225 g/8 oz whole raw tiger prawns
750 ml/1¼ pint fish stock
finely grated rind and juice of 1 lime
1 tbsp fish sauce
1 red chilli, deseeded and chopped
1 tbsp soy sauce
1 lemon grass stalk
2 tbsp rice vinegar
4 tbsp freshly chopped coriander

1 To make spring onion curls, finely shred the spring onions lengthways. Place in a bowl of iced cold water and reserve.

2 Remove the heads and shells from the prawns leaving the tails intact.

3 Split the prawns almost in two to form a butterfly shape and individually remove the black thread that runs down the back of each one.

4 In a large pan heat the stock with the lime rind and juice, fish sauce, chilli and soy sauce.

5 Bruise the lemon grass by crushing it along its length with a rolling pin, then add to the stock mixture.

6 When the stock mixture is boiling add the prawns and cook until they are pink.

7 Remove the lemon grass and add the rice vinegar and coriander.

8 Ladle into bowls and garnish with the spring onion curls. Serve immediately.

TASTY TIP

For a more substantial dish, cook 50–75 g/2–3 oz Thai fragrant rice for 12–15 minutes, or until just cooked. Drain, then place a little in the soup bowl and ladle the prepared soup on top.

1

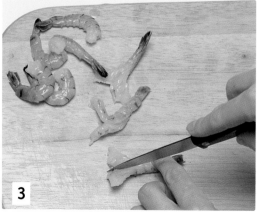

3

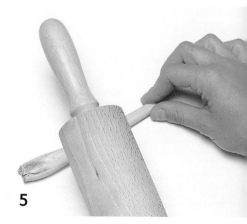

5

Curried Parsnip Soup

INGREDIENTS

Serves 4

1 tsp cumin seeds
2 tsp coriander seeds
1 tsp oil
1 onion, peeled and chopped
1 garlic clove, peeled and crushed
$\frac{1}{2}$ tsp turmeric
$\frac{1}{4}$ tsp chilli powder
1 cinnamon stick
450 g/1 lb parsnips, peeled and
   chopped
1 litre/1$\frac{3}{4}$ pint vegetable stock
salt and freshly ground black pepper
2–3 tbsp low-fat natural yogurt,
   to serve
fresh coriander leaves, to garnish

FOOD FACT

Parsnips vary in colour from pale yellow to a creamy white. They are at their best when they are the size of a large carrot. If larger, remove the central core which can be woody.

1 In a small frying pan, dry-fry the cumin and coriander seeds over a moderately high heat for 1–2 minutes. Shake the pan during cooking until the seeds are lightly toasted.

2 Reserve until cooled. Grind the toasted seeds in a pestle and mortar.

3 Heat the oil in a saucepan. Cook the onion until softened and starting to turn golden.

4 Add the garlic, turmeric, chilli powder and cinnamon stick to the pan. Continue to cook for a further minute.

5 Add the parsnips and stir well. Pour in the stock and bring to the boil. Cover and simmer for 15 minutes or until the parsnips are cooked.

6 Allow the soup to cool. Once cooled, remove the cinnamon stick and discard.

7 Blend the soup in a food processor until very smooth.

8 Transfer to a saucepan and reheat gently. Season to taste with salt and pepper. Garnish with fresh coriander and serve immediately with the yogurt.

Mushroom & Red Wine Pâté

INGREDIENTS

Serves 4

3 large slices of white bread,
  crusts removed
2 tsp oil
1 small onion, peeled and
  finely chopped
1 garlic clove, peeled and crushed
350 g/12 oz button mushrooms,
  wiped and finely chopped
150 ml/¼ pint red wine
½ tsp dried mixed herbs
1 tbsp freshly chopped parsley
salt and freshly ground black pepper
2 tbsp low-fat cream cheese

To serve:
finely chopped cucumber
finely chopped tomato

1. Preheat the oven to 180°C/ 350°F/Gas Mark 4. Cut the bread in half diagonally. Place the bread triangles on a baking tray and cook for 10 minutes.

2. Remove from the oven and split each bread triangle in half to make 12 triangles and return to the oven until golden and crisp. Leave to cool on a wire rack.

3. Heat the oil in a saucepan and gently cook the onion and garlic until transparent.

4. Add the mushrooms and cook, stirring for 3–4 minutes or until the mushroom juices start to run.

5. Stir the wine and herbs into the mushroom mixture and bring to the boil. Reduce the heat and simmer uncovered until all the liquid is absorbed.

6. Remove from the heat and season to taste with salt and pepper. Leave to cool.

7. When cold, beat in the soft cream cheese and adjust the seasoning. Place in a small clean bowl and chill until required. Serve the toast triangles with the cucumber and tomato.

TASTY TIP

This pâté is also delicious served as a bruschetta topping. Toast slices of ciabatta, generously spread the pâté on top and garnish with a little rocket.

1

5

7

Thai Fish Cakes

INGREDIENTS

Serves 4

1 red chilli, deseeded and
  roughly chopped
4 tbsp roughly chopped
  fresh coriander
1 garlic clove, peeled and crushed
2 spring onions, trimmed and
  roughly chopped
1 lemon grass, outer leaves discarded
  and roughly chopped
75 g/3 oz prawns, thawed if frozen
275 g/10 oz cod fillet, skinned, pin
  bones removed and cubed
salt and freshly ground black pepper
sweet chilli dipping sauce, to serve

TASTY TIP

A horseradish accompaniment could be used in place of the sweet chilli sauce if a creamier dip is preferred. Mix together 2 tablespoons of grated horseradish (from a jar) with 3 tablespoons each of Greek yogurt and low-calorie mayonnaise. Add 3 finely chopped spring onions, a squeeze of lime and salt and pepper to taste.

1 Preheat the oven to 190°C/375°F/Gas Mark 5. Place the chilli, coriander, garlic, spring onions and lemon grass in a food processor and blend together.

2 Pat the prawns and cod dry with kitchen paper.

3 Add to the food processor and blend until the mixture is roughly chopped.

4 Season to taste with salt and pepper and blend to mix.

5 Dampen the hands, then shape heaped tablespoons of the mixture into 12 little patties.

6 Place the patties on a lightly oiled baking sheet and cook in the preheated oven for 12–15 minutes or until piping hot and cooked through. Turn the patties over halfway through the cooking time.

7 Serve the fish cakes immediately with the sweet chilli sauce for dipping.

1

2

5

Hoisin Chicken Pancakes

INGREDIENTS

Serves 4

3 tbsp hoisin sauce

1 garlic clove, peeled and crushed

2.5 cm/1 inch piece root ginger,
  peeled and finely grated

1 tbsp soy sauce

1 tsp sesame oil

salt and freshly ground black pepper

4 skinless chicken thighs

½ cucumber, peeled (optional)

12 bought Chinese pancakes

6 spring onions, trimmed and cut
  lengthways into fine shreds

sweet chilli dipping sauce, to serve

TASTY TIP

For those with wheat allergies or who want to make this tasty dish more substantial, stir-fry the spring onions and cucumber batons in a little groundnut oil. Add a carrot cut into batons and mix in the thinly sliced chicken and reserved marinade (as prepared in step 3). Serve with steamed rice – Thai fragrant rice is particularly good.

1 Preheat the oven to 190°C/375°F/Gas Mark 5. In a non-metallic bowl, mix the hoisin sauce with the garlic, ginger, soy sauce, sesame oil and seasoning.

2 Add the chicken thighs and turn to coat in the mixture. Cover loosely and leave in the refrigerator to marinate for 3–4 hours, turning the chicken from time to time.

3 Remove the chicken from the marinade and place in a roasting tin. Reserve the marinade. Bake in the preheated oven for 30 minutes basting occasionally with the marinade.

4 Cut the cucumber in half lengthways and remove the seeds by running a teaspoon down the middle to scoop them out. Cut into thin batons.

5 Place the pancakes in a steamer to warm or heat according to packet instructions. Thinly slice the hot chicken and arrange on a plate with the shredded spring onions, cucumber and pancakes.

6 Place a spoonful of the chicken in the middle of each warmed pancake and top with pieces of cucumber, spring onion, and a little dipping sauce. Roll up and serve immediately.

2

4

5

Roasted Red Pepper, Tomato & Red Onion Soup

INGREDIENTS

Serves 4

fine spray of oil

2 large red peppers, deseeded and
   roughly chopped

1 red onion, peeled and
   roughly chopped

350 g/12 oz tomatoes, halved

1 small crusty French loaf

1 garlic clove, peeled

600 ml/1 pint vegetable stock

salt and freshly ground black pepper

1 tsp Worcestershire sauce

4 tbsp half-fat fromage frais

HELPFUL HINT

A quick hassle-free way to remove the skin from peppers once they have been roasted or grilled is to place them in a polythene bag. Leave for 10 minutes or until cool enough to handle, then simply peel the skin away from the flesh.

1   Preheat the oven to 190°C/375°F/Gas Mark 5. Spray a large roasting tin with the oil and place the peppers and onion in the base. Cook in the oven for 10 minutes. Add the tomatoes and cook for a further 20 minutes or until the peppers are soft.

2   Cut the bread into 1 cm/½ inch slices. Cut the garlic clove in half and rub the cut edge of the garlic over the bread.

3   Place all the bread slices on a large baking tray, and bake in the preheated oven for 10 minutes, turning halfway through, until golden and crisp.

4   Remove the vegetables from the oven and allow to cool slightly, then blend in a food processor until smooth. Strain the vegetable mixture through a large nylon sieve into a saucepan, to remove the seeds and skin. Add the stock, season to taste with salt and pepper and stir to mix. Heat the soup gently until piping hot.

5   In a small bowl beat together the Worcestershire sauce with the fromage frais.

6   Pour the soup into warmed bowls and swirl a spoonful of the fromage frais mixture into each bowl. Serve immediately with the garlic toasts.

1

4

5

Hot Herby Mushrooms

INGREDIENTS

Serves 4

4 thin slices of white bread,
  crusts removed
125 g/4 oz chestnut mushrooms,
  wiped and sliced
125 g/4 oz oyster mushrooms, wiped
1 garlic clove, peeled and crushed
1 tsp Dijon mustard
300 ml/½ pint chicken stock
  salt and freshly ground black pepper
1 tbsp freshly chopped parsley
1 tbsp freshly snipped chives, plus
  extra to garnish
mixed salad leaves, to serve

FOOD FACT

Mushrooms are an extremely nutritious food, rich in vitamins and minerals, which help to boost our immune system. This recipe could be adapted to include shiitake mushrooms which studies have shown can significantly boost and protect the body's immune system and can go some way to boost the body's protection against cancer.

1 Preheat the oven to 180°C/350°F/Gas Mark 4. With a rolling pin, roll each piece of bread out as thinly as possible.

2 Press each piece of bread into a 10 cm/4 inch tartlet tin. Push each piece firmly down, then bake in the preheated oven for 20 minutes.

3 Place the mushrooms in a frying pan with the garlic, mustard and chicken stock and stir-fry over a moderate heat until the mushrooms are tender and the liquid is reduced by half.

4 Carefully remove the mushrooms from the frying pan with a slotted spoon and transfer to a heat-resistant dish. Cover with tinfoil and place in the bottom of the oven to keep the mushrooms warm.

5 Boil the remaining pan juices until reduced to a thick sauce. Season with salt and pepper.

6 Stir the parsley and the chives into the mushroom mixture.

7 Place one bread tartlet case on each plate and divide the mushroom mixture between them.

8 Spoon over the pan juices, garnish with the chives and serve immediately with mixed salad leaves.

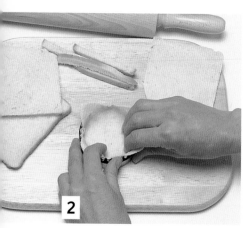
2

3

5

Coriander Chicken & Soy Sauce Cakes

INGREDIENTS

Serves 4

¼ cucumber, peeled

1 shallot, peeled and thinly sliced

6 radishes, trimmed and sliced

350 g/12 oz skinless boneless
   chicken thigh

4 tbsp roughly chopped
   fresh coriander

2 spring onions, trimmed and
   roughly chopped

1 red chilli, deseeded and chopped

finely grated rind of ½ lime

2 tbsp soy sauce

1 tbsp caster sugar

2 tbsp rice vinegar

1 red chilli, deseeded and finely sliced

freshly chopped coriander, to garnish

FOOD FACT

In this recipe, the chicken cakes
can be altered so that half chicken
and half lean pork is used. This
alters the flavour of the dish and
works really well if a small 2.5 cm/
1 inch piece of fresh ginger is
grated and added in step 4.

1 Preheat the oven to 190°C/375°F/Gas Mark 5. Halve the cucumber lengthways, deseed and dice.

2 In a bowl mix the shallot and radishes. Chill until ready to serve with the diced cucumber.

3 Place the chicken thighs in a food processor and blend until coarsely chopped.

4 Add the coriander and spring onions to the chicken with the chilli, lime rind and soy sauce. Blend again until mixed.

5 Using slightly damp hands, shape the chicken mixture into 12 small rounds.

6 Place the rounds on a lightly oiled baking tray and bake in the preheated for 15 minutes, until golden.

7 In a small pan heat the sugar with 2 tablespoons of water until dissolved. Simmer until syrupy.

8 Remove from the heat and allow to cool a little, then stir in the vinegar and chilli slices. Pour over the cucumber and the radish and shallot salad. Garnish with the chopped coriander and serve the chicken cakes with the salad immediately.

2

4

6

Roasted Aubergine Dip with Pitta Strips

INGREDIENTS

Serves 4

4 pitta breads
2 large aubergines
1 garlic clove, peeled
¼ tsp sesame oil
1 tbsp lemon juice
½ tsp ground cumin
salt and freshly ground black pepper
2 tbsp freshly chopped parsley
fresh salad leaves, to serve

FOOD FACT

This dish is a variation on the traditional Arabic dish known as Baba Ganoush, which translates to spoilt old man. As well as being great with pitta strips or bread sticks, this dish is fantastic warmed through and served as a meal accompaniment.

1 Preheat the oven to 180°C/350°F/Gas Mark 4. On a chopping board cut the pitta breads into strips. Spread the bread in a single layer on to a large baking tray.

2 Cook in the preheated oven for 15 minutes until golden and crisp. Leave to cool on a wire cooling rack.

3 Trim the aubergines, rinse lightly and reserve. Heat a griddle pan until almost smoking. Cook the aubergines and garlic for about 15 minutes.

4 Turn the aubergines frequently, until very tender with wrinkled and charred skins. Remove from heat. Leave to cool.

5 When the aubergines are cool enough to handle, cut in half and scoop out the cooked flesh and place in a food processor.

6 Squeeze the softened garlic flesh from the papery skin and add to the aubergine.

7 Blend the aubergine and garlic until smooth, then add the sesame oil, lemon juice and cumin and blend again to mix.

8 Season to taste with salt and pepper, stir in the parsley and serve with the pitta strips and mixed salad leaves.

3

6

7

Griddled Garlic & Lemon Squid

INGREDIENTS

Serves 4

125 g/4 oz long-grain rice
300 ml/½ pint fish stock
225 g/8 oz squid, cleaned
finely grated rind of 1 lemon
1 garlic clove, peeled and crushed
1 shallot, peeled and finely chopped
2 tbsp freshly chopped coriander
2 tbsp lemon juice
salt and freshly ground black pepper

HELPFUL HINT

To prepare squid, peel the tentacles from the squid's pouch and cut away the head just below the eye. Discard the head. Remove the quill and the soft innards from the squid and discard. Peel off any dark skin that covers the squid and discard. Rinse the tentacles and pouch thoroughly. The squid is now ready to use.

1   Rinse the rice until the water runs clear, then place in a saucepan with the stock.

2   Bring to the boil, then reduce the heat. Cover and simmer gently for 10 minutes.

3   Turn off the heat and leave the pan covered so the rice can steam while you cook the squid.

4   Remove the tentacles from the squid and reserve.

5   Cut the body cavity in half. Using the tip of a small sharp knife, score the inside flesh of the body cavity in a diamond pattern. Do not cut all the way through.

6   Mix the lemon rind, crushed garlic and chopped shallot together.

7   Place the squid in a shallow bowl and sprinkle over the lemon mixture and stir.

8   Heat a griddle pan until almost smoking. Cook the squid for 3–4 minutes until cooked through, then slice.

9   Sprinkle with the coriander and lemon juice. Season to taste with salt and pepper. Drain the rice and serve immediately with the squid.

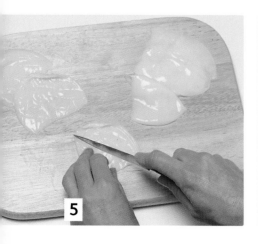

5

7

8

Creamy Salmon with Dill in Filo Baskets

INGREDIENTS

Serves 4

1 bay leaf
6 black peppercorns
1 large sprig fresh parsley
175 g/6 oz salmon fillet
4 large sheets filo pastry
fine spray of oil
125 g/4 oz baby spinach leaves
8 tbsp low-fat fromage frais
2 tsp Dijon mustard
2 tbsp freshly chopped dill
salt and freshly ground black pepper

FOOD FACT

This is a highly nutritious dish combining calcium-rich salmon with vitamin and mineral-rich spinach. The low-fat fromage frais in this recipe can be substituted for low-fat live yogurt if you want to aid digestion and give the immune system a real boost!

1 Preheat the oven to 200°C/400°F/Gas Mark 6. Place the bay leaf, peppercorns, parsley and salmon in a frying pan and add enough water to barely cover the fish.

2 Bring to the boil, reduce the heat and poach the fish for 5 minutes until it flakes easily. Remove it from the pan. Reserve.

3 Spray each sheet of filo pastry lightly with the oil. Scrunch up the pastry to make a nest shape approximately 12.5 cm/5 inches in diameter.

4 Place on a lightly oiled baking sheet and cook in the preheated oven for 10 minutes until golden and crisp.

5 Blanch the spinach in a pan of lightly salted boiling water for 2 minutes. Drain thoroughly and keep warm.

6 Mix the fromage frais, mustard and dill together, then warm gently. Season to taste with salt and pepper. Divide the spinach between the filo pastry nests and flake the salmon on to the spinach.

7 Spoon the mustard and dill sauce over the filo baskets and serve immediately.

1

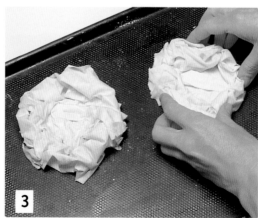
3

6

Smoked Salmon Sushi

INGREDIENTS

Serves 4

175 g/6 oz sushi rice
2 tbsp rice vinegar
4 tsp caster sugar
½ tsp salt
2 sheets sushi nori
60 g/2½ oz smoked salmon
¼ cucumber, cut into fine strips

To serve:
wasabi
soy sauce
pickled ginger

1 Rinse the rice thoroughly in cold water, until the water runs clear, then place in a pan with 300 ml/½ pint of water. Bring to the boil and cover with a tight-fitting lid. Reduce to a simmer and cook gently for 10 minutes. Turn the heat off, but keep the pan covered, to allow the rice to steam for a further 10 minutes.

2 In a small saucepan gently heat the rice vinegar, sugar and salt until the sugar has dissolved. When the rice has finished steaming, pour over the vinegar mixture and stir well to mix. Empty the rice out on to a large flat surface (a chopping board or large plate is ideal). Fan the rice to cool and to produce a shinier rice.

3 Lay one sheet of sushi nori on a sushi mat (if you do not have a sushi mat, improvise with a stiff piece of fabric that is a little larger than the sushi nori) and spread with half the cooled rice. Dampen the hands while doing this (this helps to prevent the rice from sticking to the hands). On the nearest edge place half the salmon and half the cucumber strips.

4 Roll up the rice and smoked salmon into a tight Swiss roll-like shape. Dampen the blade of a sharp knife and cut the sushi into slices about 2 cm/¾ inch thick. Repeat with the remaining sushi nori, rice, smoked salmon and cucumber. Serve with wasabi, soy sauce and pickled ginger.

TASTY TIP
If wasabi is unavailable, use a little horseradish. If unable to get sushi nori (seaweed sheets), shape the rice into small bite-size oblongs, then drape a piece of smoked salmon over each one and garnish with chives.

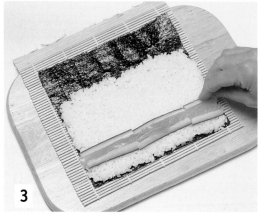

Honey & Ginger Prawns

INGREDIENTS

Serves 4

1 carrot

50 g/2 oz bamboo shoots

4 spring onions

1 tbsp clear honey

1 tbsp tomato ketchup

1 tsp soy sauce

2.5 cm/1 inch piece fresh root ginger, peeled and finely grated

1 garlic clove, peeled and crushed

1 tbsp lime juice

175 g/6 oz peeled prawns, thawed if frozen

2 heads little gem lettuce leaves

2 tbsp freshly chopped coriander

salt and freshly ground black pepper

To garnish:

fresh coriander sprigs

lime slices

HELPFUL HINT

If liked, raw tiger prawns can be used for this recipe – do make sure if using raw prawns that the black vein that runs along their back is removed.

1 Cut the carrot into matchstick-size pieces, roughly chop the bamboo shoots and finely slice the spring onions.

2 Combine the bamboo shoots with the carrot matchsticks and spring onions.

3 In a wok or large frying pan gently heat the honey, tomato ketchup, soy sauce, ginger, garlic and lime juice with 3 tablespoons of water. Bring to the boil.

4 Add the carrot mixture and stir-fry for 2–3 minutes until the vegetables are hot.

5 Add the prawns and continue to stir-fry for 2 minutes.

6 Remove the wok or frying pan from the heat and reserve until cooled slightly.

7 Divide the little gem lettuce into leaves and rinse lightly.

8 Stir the chopped coriander into the prawn mixture and season to taste with salt and pepper. Spoon into the lettuce leaves and serve immediately garnished with sprigs of fresh coriander and lime slices.

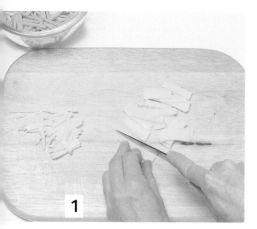

1

5

8

Tuna Chowder

INGREDIENTS

Serves 4

2 tsp oil
1 onion, peeled and finely chopped
2 sticks of celery, trimmed and
   finely sliced
1 tbsp plain flour
600 ml/1 pint skimmed milk
200 g can tuna in water
320 g can sweetcorn in water, drained
2 tsp freshly chopped thyme
salt and freshly ground black pepper
pinch cayenne pepper
2 tbsp freshly chopped parsley

TASTY TIP

This creamy soup also works well using equivalent amounts of canned crab meat instead of the tuna. For a contrasting taste and to enhance the delicate creaminess of this soup, add a spoonful of low-fat crème fraîche to the top of the soup. Sprinkle with cayenne pepper and then garnish with a few long chive leaves.

1 Heat the oil in a large heavy-based saucepan. Add the onion and celery and gently cook for about 5 minutes, stirring from time to time until the onion is softened.

2 Stir in the flour and cook for about 1 minute to thicken.

3 Draw the pan off the heat and gradually pour in the milk, stirring throughout.

4 Add the tuna and its liquid, the drained sweetcorn and the thyme.

5 Mix gently, then bring to the boil. Cover and simmer for 5 minutes.

6 Remove the pan from the heat and season to taste with salt and pepper.

7 Sprinkle the chowder with the cayenne pepper and chopped parsley. Divide into soup bowls and serve immediately.

Oriental Minced Chicken on Rocket & Tomato

INGREDIENTS

Serves 4

2 shallots, peeled
1 garlic clove, peeled
1 carrot, peeled
50 g/2 oz water chestnuts
1 tsp oil
350 g/12 oz fresh chicken mince
1 tsp Chinese 5-spice powder
pinch chilli powder
1 tsp soy sauce
1 tbsp fish sauce
8 cherry tomatoes
50 g/2 oz rocket

TASTY TIP

In place of the chicken you could use any lean cut of meat or even prawns. To make this dish a main meal replace the rocket and tomatoes with stir-fried vegetables and rice. Another alternative is to serve the chicken mixture in step 3 in lettuce leaves. Place a spoonful of the mixture into a lettuce leaf and roll up into a small parcel.

1 Finely chop the shallots and garlic. Cut the carrot into matchsticks, thinly slice the water chestnuts and reserve. Heat the oil in a wok or heavy-based large frying pan and add the chicken. Stir-fry for 3–4 minutes over a moderately high heat, breaking up any large pieces of chicken.

2 Add the garlic and shallots and cook for 2–3 minutes until softened. Sprinkle over the Chinese 5-spice powder and the chilli powder and continue to cook for about 1 minute.

3 Add the carrot, water chestnuts, soy and fish sauce and 2 tablespoons of water. Stir-fry for a further 2 minutes. Remove from the heat and reserve to cool slightly.

4 Deseed the tomatoes and cut into thin wedges. Toss with the rocket and divide between 4 serving plates. Spoon the warm chicken mixture over the rocket and tomato wedges and serve immediately to prevent the rocket from wilting.

1

1

4

Gingered Cod Steaks

INGREDIENTS

Serves 4

2.5 cm/1 inch piece fresh root
ginger, peeled
4 spring onions
2 tsp freshly chopped parsley
1 tbsp soft brown sugar
4 x 175 g/6 oz thick cod steaks
salt and freshly ground black pepper
25 g/1 oz half-fat butter
freshly cooked vegetables, to serve

TASTY TIP

Why not serve this dish with roasted new potatoes en papillote. Place the new potatoes into double thickness greaseproof paper with a few cloves of peeled garlic. Drizzle with a little olive oil and season well with salt and black pepper. Fold all the edges of the greaseproof paper together and roast in the oven at 180°C/350°F/Gas Mark 4 for 40–50 minutes before serving in the paper casing.

1 Preheat the grill and line the grill rack with a layer of tinfoil. Coarsely grate the piece of ginger. Trim the spring onions and cut into thin strips.

2 Mix the spring onions, ginger, chopped parsley and sugar. Add 1 tablespoon of water.

3 Wipe the fish steaks. Season to taste with salt and pepper. Place on to 4 separate 20.5 x 20.5 cm/8 x 8 inch tinfoil squares.

4 Carefully spoon the spring onions and ginger mixture over the fish.

5 Cut the butter into small cubes and place over the fish.

6 Loosely fold the foil over the steaks to enclose the fish and to make a parcel.

7 Place under the preheated grill and cook for 10–12 minutes or until cooked and the flesh has turned opaque.

8 Place the fish parcels on individual serving plates. Serve immediately with the freshly cooked vegetables.

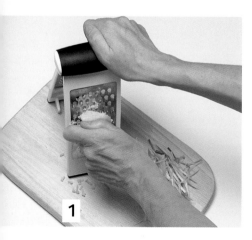

1

3

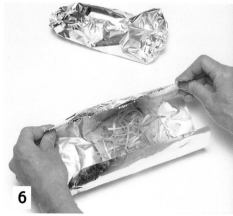

6

Seared Pancetta-wrapped Cod

INGREDIENTS

Serves 4

4 x 175 g/6 oz thick cod fillets
4 very thin slices of pancetta
3 tbsp capers in vinegar
1 tbsp of vegetable or sunflower oil
2 tbsp lemon juice
1 tbsp olive oil
freshly ground black pepper
1 tbsp freshly chopped parsley,
 to garnish

To serve:

freshly cooked vegetables
new potatoes

FOOD FACT

Pancetta is Italian-cured belly pork, which is often delicately smoked and sold either finely sliced or chopped roughly into small cubes. The slices of pancetta can be used to encase poultry and fish, whereas chopped pancetta is often used in sauces. To cook chopped pancetta fry for 2–3 minutes and reserve. Use the oil to seal meat or to fry onions, then return the pancetta to the pan.

1 Wipe the cod fillets and wrap each one with the pancetta. Secure each fillet with a cocktail stick and reserve.

2 Drain the capers and soak in cold water for 10 minutes to remove any excess salt, then drain and reserve.

3 Heat the oil in a large frying pan and sear the wrapped pieces of cod fillet for about 3 minutes on each side, turning carefully with a fish slice so as not to break up the fish.

4 Lower the heat then continue to cook for 2–3 minutes or until the fish is cooked thoroughly.

5 Meanwhile, place the reserved capers, lemon juice and olive oil into a small saucepan. Grind over the black pepper.

6 Place the saucepan over a low heat and bring to a gentle simmer, stirring continuously for 2–3 minutes.

7 Once the fish is cooked, garnish with the parsley and serve with the warm caper dressing, freshly cooked vegetables and new potatoes.

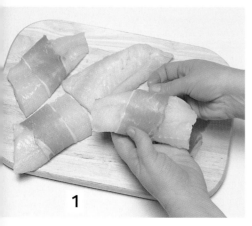

1

3

6

Mussels Linguine

INGREDIENTS

Serves 4

2 kg/4½ lb fresh mussels, washed
   and scrubbed
knob of butter
1 onion, peeled and finely chopped
300 ml/½ pint medium dry
   white wine

For the sauce:

1 tbsp sunflower oil
4 baby onions, peeled and quartered
2 garlic cloves, peeled and crushed
400 g can chopped tomatoes
large pinch of salt
225 g/8 oz dried linguine or tagliatelle
2 tbsp freshly chopped parsley

TASTY TIP

Serving mussels in their shells is a fantastic way to eat them. Every mussel is surrounded with the delicious sauce, adding flavour to every mouthful. Clams, which often have a sweeter flavour, could also be used in this recipe.

1 Soak the mussels in plenty of cold water. Leave in the refrigerator until required. When ready to use, scrub the mussel shells, removing any barnacles or beards. Discard any open mussels.

2 Melt the butter in a large pan. Add the mussels, onion and wine. Cover with a close-fitting lid and steam for 5–6 minutes, shaking the pan gently to ensure even cooking. Discard any mussels that have not opened, then strain and reserve the liquor.

3 To make the sauce, heat the oil in a medium-sized saucepan, and gently fry the quartered onion and garlic for 3–4 minutes until soft and transparent. Stir in the tomatoes and half the reserved mussel liquor. Bring to the boil and simmer for 7–10 minutes until the sauce begins to thicken.

4 Cook the pasta in boiling salted water for 7 minutes or or until al dente. Drain the pasta, reserving 2 tablespoons of the cooking liquor, then return the pasta and liquor to the pan.

5 Remove the meat from half the mussel shells. Stir into the sauce along with the remaining mussels. Pour the hot sauce over the cooked pasta and toss gently. Garnish with the parsley and serve immediately.

1

2

5

Barbecued Fish Kebabs

INGREDIENTS

Serves 4

450 g/1 lb herring or mackerel fillets,
  cut into chunks
2 small red onions, peeled
  and quartered
16 cherry tomatoes
salt and freshly ground black pepper

For the sauce:

150 ml/¼ pint fish stock
5 tbsp tomato ketchup
2 tbsp Worcestershire sauce
2 tbsp wine vinegar
2 tbsp brown sugar
2 drops Tabasco
2 tbsp tomato purée

TASTY TIP

Instead of cooking indoors, cook these kebabs on the barbecue for a delicious charcoaled flavour. Light the barbecue at least 20 minutes before use in order to allow the coals to heat up. Barbecue some peppers and red onions and serve with a mixed salad as an accompaniment to the fish kebabs.

1 Line a grill rack with a single layer of tinfoil and preheat the grill at a high temperature, 2 minutes before use.

2 If using wooden skewers, soak in cold water for 30 minutes to prevent them from catching alight during cooking.

3 Meanwhile, prepare the sauce. Add the fish stock, tomato ketchup, Worcestershire sauce, vinegar, sugar, Tabasco and tomato purée to a small saucepan. Stir well and leave to simmer for 5 minutes.

4 When ready to cook, drain the skewers, if necessary, then thread the fish chunks, the quartered red onions and the cherry tomatoes alternately on to the skewers.

5 Season the kebabs to taste with salt and pepper and brush with the sauce. Grill under the preheated grill for 8–10 minutes, basting with the sauce occasionally during cooking. Turn the kebabs often to ensure that they are cooked thoroughly and evenly on all sides. Serve immediately with couscous.

3

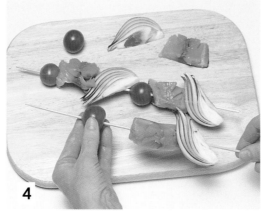

4

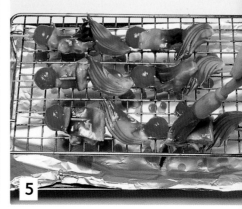

5

Ratatouille Mackerel

INGREDIENTS

Serves 4

1 red pepper
1 tbsp olive oil
1 red onion, peeled
1 garlic clove, peeled and thinly sliced
2 courgettes, trimmed and cut into
  thick slices
400 g can chopped tomatoes
sea salt and freshly ground
  black pepper
4 x 275 g/10 oz small mackerel,
  cleaned and heads removed
spray of olive oil
lemon juice for drizzling
12 fresh basil leaves
couscous or rice mixed with chopped
  parsley, to serve

1 Preheat the oven to 190°C/375°F/Gas Mark 5. Cut the top off the red pepper, remove the seeds and membrane, then cut into chunks. Cut the red onion into thick wedges.

2 Heat the oil in a large pan and cook the onion and garlic for 5 minutes or until beginning to soften.

3 Add the pepper chunks and courgette slices and cook for a further 5 minutes.

4 Pour in the chopped tomatoes with their juice and cook for a further 5 minutes. Season to taste with salt and pepper and pour into an ovenproof dish.

5 Season the fish with salt and pepper and arrange on top of the vegetables. Spray with a little olive oil and lemon juice. Cover and cook in the preheated oven for 20 minutes.

6 Remove the cover, add the basil leaves and return to the oven for a further 5 minutes. Serve immediately with couscous or rice mixed with parsley.

FOOD FACT

Ratatouille is a traditional French dish using onions, tomatoes, courgettes and often aubergine. It is a very versatile dish to which many other vegetables can be added. For that extra kick, why not add a little chopped chilli.

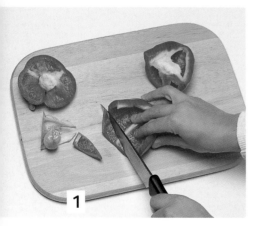

1

2

4

Cod with Fennel & Cardamom

INGREDIENTS

Serves 4

1 garlic clove, peeled and crushed
finely grated rind of 1 lemon
1 tsp lemon juice
1 tbsp olive oil
1 fennel bulb
1 tbsp cardamom pods
salt and freshly ground black pepper
4 x 175 g/6 oz thick cod fillets

FOOD FACT

When buying fresh fish, look for fish that does not smell. Any ammonia-type smelling fish should be avoided. The flesh should be plump and firm-looking. The eyes should be bright, not sunken. If in doubt, choose frozen fish. This is cleaned and packed almost as soon as it is caught. It is often fresher and contains more nutrients than its fresh counterparts.

1 Preheat the oven to 190°C/375°F/Gas Mark 5. Place the garlic in a small bowl with the lemon rind, juice and olive oil and stir well.

2 Cover and leave to infuse for at least 30 minutes. Stir well before using.

3 Trim the fennel bulb, thinly slice and place in a bowl.

4 Place the cardamom pods in a pestle and mortar and lightly pound to crack the pods.

5 Alternatively place in a polythene bag and pound gently with a rolling pin. Add the crushed cardamom to the fennel slices.

6 Season the fish with salt and pepper and place on to 4 separate 20.5 x 20.5 cm/8 x 8 inch parchment paper squares.

7 Spoon the fennel mixture over the fish and drizzle with the infused oil.

8 Place the parcels on a baking sheet and bake in the preheated oven for 8–10 minutes or until cooked. Serve immediately in the paper parcels.

1

4

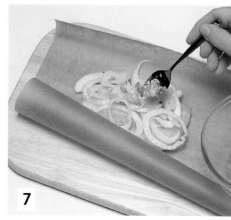

7

Seared Tuna with Pernod & Thyme

INGREDIENTS

Serves 4

4 tuna or swordfish steaks
salt and freshly ground black pepper
3 tbsp Pernod
1 tbsp olive oil
zest and juice of 1 lime
2 tsp fresh thyme leaves
4 sun-dried tomatoes

To serve:
freshly cooked mixed rice
tossed green salad

HELPFUL HINT

Tuna is now widely available all year round at fishmongers and in supermarkets. Tuna is an oily fish rich in Omega-3 fatty acids which help in the prevention of heart disease by lowering blood cholesterol levels. Tuna is usually sold in steaks, and the flesh should be dark red in colour.

1 Wipe the fish steaks with a damp cloth or dampened kitchen paper.

2 Season both sides of the fish to taste with salt and pepper, then place in a shallow bowl and reserve.

3 Mix together the Pernod, olive oil, lime zest and juice with the fresh thyme leaves.

4 Finely chop the sun-dried tomatoes and add to the Pernod mixture.

5 Pour the Pernod mixture over the fish and chill in the refrigerator for about 2 hours, spooning the marinade occasionally over the fish.

6 Heat a griddle or heavy-based frying pan. Drain the fish, reserving the marinade. Cook the fish for 3–4 minutes on each side for a steak that is still slightly pink in the middle. Or, if liked, cook the fish for 1–2 minutes longer on each side if you prefer your fish cooked through.

7 Place the remaining marinade in a small saucepan and bring to the boil. Pour the marinade over the fish and serve immediately, with the mixed rice and salad.

2

5

6

Haddock with an Olive Crust

INGREDIENTS

Serves 4

12 pitted black olives, finely chopped
75 g/3 oz fresh white breadcrumbs
1 tbsp freshly chopped tarragon
1 garlic clove, peeled and crushed
3 spring onions, trimmed and
  finely chopped
1 tbsp olive oil
4 x 175 g/6 oz thick skinless
  haddock fillets

To serve:

freshly cooked carrots
freshly cooked beans

1   Preheat the oven to 190°C/375°F/Gas Mark 5. Place the black olives in a small bowl with the breadcrumbs and add the chopped tarragon.

2   Add the garlic to the olives with the chopped spring onions and the olive oil. Mix together lightly.

3   Wipe the fillets with either a clean damp cloth or damp kitchen paper, then place on a lightly oiled baking sheet.

4   Place spoonfuls of the olive and breadcrumb mixture on top of each fillet and press the mixture down lightly and evenly over the top of the fish.

5   Bake the fish in the preheated oven for 20–25 minutes or until the fish is cooked thoroughly and the topping is golden brown. Serve immediately with the freshly cooked carrots and beans.

TASTY TIP

Why not try experimenting by adding other ingredients to the crust. Adding 2 cloves of roasted garlic gives the crust a delicious flavour. Simply mash the garlic and add to the crumbs. Also, a combination of white and wholemeal breadcrumbs can be used for a nuttier, malty taste.

2

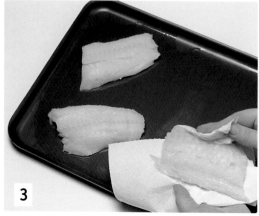
3

4

Citrus Monkfish Kebabs

INGREDIENTS

Serves 4

Marinade:

1 tbsp sunflower oil
finely grated rind and juice of 1 lime
1 tbsp lemon juice
1 sprig of freshly chopped rosemary
1 tbsp whole-grain mustard
1 garlic clove, peeled and crushed
salt and freshly ground black pepper

For the kebabs:

450 g/1 lb monkfish tail
8 raw tiger prawns
1 small green courgette, trimmed
  and sliced
4 tbsp of half-fat crème fraîche

1 Preheat the grill and line the grill rack with tinfoil. Mix all the marinade ingredients together in a small bowl and reserve.

2 Using a sharp knife, cut down both sides of the monkfish tail. Remove the bone and discard. Cut away and discard any skin, then cut the monkfish into bite-sized cubes.

3 Peel the prawns, leaving the tails intact and remove the thin black vein that runs down the back of each prawn. Place the fish and prawns in a shallow dish.

4 Pour the marinade over the fish and prawns. Cover lightly and leave to marinate in the refrigerator for 30 minutes. Spoon the marinade over the fish and prawns occasionally during this time. Soak the skewers in cold water for 30 minutes, then drain.

5 Thread the cubes of fish, prawns and courgettes on to the drained skewers.

6 Arrange on the grill rack then place under the preheated grill and cook for 5–7 minutes, or until cooked thoroughly and the prawns have turned pink. Occasionally brush with the remaining marinade and turn the kebabs during cooking.

7 Mix 2 tablespoons of the marinade with the crème fraîche and serve as a dip with the kebabs.

FOOD FACT

Monkfish is so versatile. It can be roasted in the oven, poached, baked or grilled. Its firm flesh is ideal for kebabs.

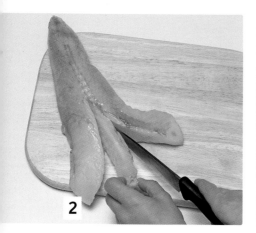

2

4

5

Sardines with Redcurrants

INGREDIENTS

Serves 4

2 tbsp redcurrant jelly
finely grated rind of 1 lime
2 tbsp medium dry sherry
450 g/1 lb fresh sardines, cleaned
  and heads removed
sea salt and freshly ground
  black pepper
lime wedges, to garnish

To serve:

fresh redcurrants
fresh green salad

COOK'S TIP

Most fish are sold cleaned but it is easy to do yourself. Using the back of a knife, scrape off the scales from the tail towards the head. Make a small slit along their bellies using a sharp knife. Carefully scrape out the entrails and rinse thoroughly under cold running water. Pat dry with absorbent paper.

1 Preheat the grill and line the grill rack with tinfoil 2–3 minutes before cooking.

2 Warm the redcurrant jelly in a bowl standing over a pan of gently simmering water and stir until smooth. Add the lime rind and sherry to the bowl and stir well until blended.

3 Lightly rinse the sardines and pat dry with absorbent kitchen paper.

4 Place on a chopping board and with a sharp knife make several diagonal cuts across the flesh of each fish. Season the sardines inside the cavities with salt and pepper.

5 Gently brush the warm marinade over the skin and inside the cavities of the sardines.

6 Place on the grill rack and cook under the preheated grill for 8–10 minutes, or until the fish are cooked.

7 Carefully turn the sardines over at least once during grilling. Baste occasionally with the remaining redcurrant and lime marinade. Garnish with the redcurrants. Serve immediately with the salad and lime wedges.

2

4

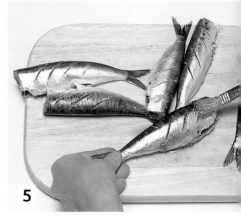

5

Hot Salsa–filled Sole

INGREDIENTS

Serves 4

8 x 175 g/6 oz lemon sole
   fillets, skinned
150 ml/¼ pint orange juice
2 tbsp lemon juice

For the salsa:

1 small mango
8 cherry tomatoes, quartered
1 small red onion, peeled and
   finely chopped
pinch of sugar
1 red chilli
2 tbsp rice vinegar
zest and juice of 1 lime
1 tbsp olive oil
sea salt and freshly ground
   black pepper
2 tbsp freshly chopped mint
lime wedges, to garnish
salad leaves, to serve

1 First make the salsa. Peel the mango and cut the flesh away from the stone. Chop finely and place in a small bowl. Add the cherry tomatoes to the mango together with the onion and sugar.

2 Cut the top of the chilli. Slit down the side and discard the seeds and the membrane (the skin to which the seeds are attached). Finely chop the chilli and add to the mango mixture with the vinegar, lime zest, juice and oil. Season to taste with salt and pepper. Mix thoroughly and leave to stand for 30 minutes to allow the flavours to develop.

3 Lay the fish fillets on a board skinned side up and pile the salsa on the tail end of the fillets. Fold the fillets in half, season and place in a large shallow frying pan. Pour over the orange and lemon juice.

4 Bring to a gentle boil, then reduce the heat to a simmer. Cover and cook on a low heat for 7–10 minutes, adding a little water if the liquid is evaporating. Remove the cover, add the mint and cook uncovered for a further 3 minutes. Garnish with lime wedges and serve immediately with the salad.

HELPFUL HINT

Sometimes the skin will burn after handling chillies. Take care not to touch the eyes, before washing the hands.

1

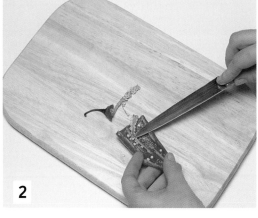

2

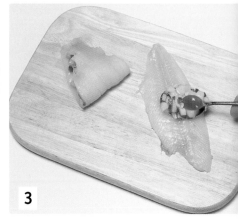

3

Smoked Haddock Rosti

INGREDIENTS

Serves 4

450 g/1 lb potatoes, peeled and
  coarsely grated
1 large onion, peeled and
  coarsely grated
2–3 garlic cloves, peeled and crushed
450 g/1 lb smoked haddock
1 tbsp olive oil
salt and freshly ground black pepper
finely grated rind of ½ lemon
1 tbsp freshly chopped parsley
2 tbsp half-fat crème fraîche
mixed salad leaves, to garnish
lemon wedges, to serve

1 Dry the grated potatoes in a clean tea towel. Rinse the grated onion thoroughly in cold water, dry in a clean tea towel and add to the potatoes.

2 Stir the garlic into the potato mixture. Skin the smoked haddock and remove as many of the tiny pin bones as possible. Cut into thin slices and reserve.

3 Heat the oil in a non-stick frying pan. Add half the potatoes and press well down in the frying pan. Season to taste with salt and pepper.

4 Add a layer of fish and a sprinkling of lemon rind, parsley and a little black pepper.

5 Top with the remaining potatoes and press down firmly. Cover with a sheet of tinfoil and cook on the lowest heat for 25–30 minutes.

6 Preheat the grill 2–3 minutes before the end of cooking time. Remove the tinfoil and place the rosti under the grill to brown. Turn out on to a warmed serving dish, and serve immediately with spoonfuls of crème fraîche, lemon wedges and mixed salad leaves.

HELPFUL HINT

Use smoked haddock fillets. Finnan or arbroath smokies would be too bony for this dish.

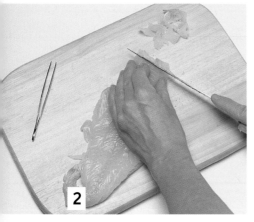

2

3

4

Sweet-&-Sour Prawns with Noodles

INGREDIENTS

Serves 4

425 g can pineapple pieces in
   natural juice
1 green pepper, deseeded and cut
   into quarters
1 tbsp groundnut oil
1 onion, cut into thin wedges
3 tbsp soft brown sugar
150 ml/¼ pint chicken stock
4 tbsp wine vinegar
1 tbsp tomato purée
1 tbsp light soy sauce
1 tbsp cornflour
350 g/12 oz raw tiger prawns, peeled
225 g/8 oz pak choi, shredded
350 g/12 oz medium egg noodles
coriander leaves, to garnish

HELPFUL HINT

This dish works well with Thai Jasmine steamed rice and also wholewheat noodles which have a more nutritional value. When using raw tiger prawns, make sure that the black vein that runs along their backs has been completely removed.

1 Make the sauce by draining the pineapple and reserving 2 tablespoons of the juice.

2 Remove the membrane from the quartered peppers and cut into thin strips.

3 Heat the oil in a saucepan. Add the onion and pepper and cook for about 4 minutes or until the onion has softened.

4 Add the pineapple, the sugar, stock, vinegar, tomato purée and the soy sauce.

5 Bring the sauce to the boil and simmer for about 4 minutes. Blend the cornflour with the reserved pineapple juice and stir into the pan, stirring until thickened.

6 Clean the prawns if needed. Wash the pak choi thoroughly, then shred.

7 Add the prawns and pak choi to the sauce. Simmer gently for 3 minutes or until the prawns are cooked and have turned pink.

8 Cook the noodles in boiling water for 4–5 minutes until just tender.

9 Drain and arrange the noodles on a warmed plate and pour over the sweet-and-sour prawns. Garnish with coriander leaves and serve immediately.

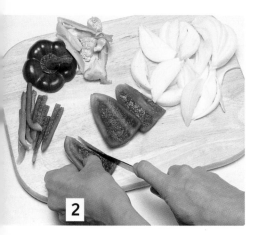

2

3

6

Salmon Fish Cakes

INGREDIENTS

Serves 4

225 g/8 oz potatoes, peeled
450 g/1 lb salmon fillet, skinned
125 g/4 oz carrot, trimmed
   and peeled
2 tbsp grated lemon rind
2–3 tbsp freshly chopped coriander
1 medium egg yolk
salt and freshly ground black pepper
2 tbsp plain white flour
few fine sprays of oil

To serve:
prepared tomato sauce
tossed green salad
crusty bread

FOOD FACT

Salmon is now easily affordable due to salmon farming. It is readily available all-year-round and is often cheaper to buy than cod. It is an excellent source of Omega-3 fatty acids which help lower blood cholesterol levels.

1 Cube the potatoes and cook in lightly salted boiling water for 15 minutes. Drain and mash the potatoes. Place in a mixing bowl and reserve.

2 Place the salmon in a food processor and blend to form a chunky purée. Add the purée to the potatoes and mix together.

3 Coarsely grate the carrot and add to the fish with the lemon rind and the coriander.

4 Add the egg yolk, season to taste with salt and pepper, then gently mix the ingredients together. With damp hands form the mixture into 4 large fish cakes.

5 Coat in the flour and place on a plate. Cover loosely and chill for at least 30 minutes.

6 When ready to cook, spray a griddle pan with a few fine sprays of oil and heat the pan. When hot add the fish cakes and cook on both sides for 3–4 minutes or until the fish is cooked. Add an extra spray of oil if needed during the cooking.

7 When the fish cakes are cooked, serve immediately with the tomato sauce, green salad and crusty bread.

2

4

6

Citrus–grilled Plaice

INGREDIENTS

Serves 4

1 tsp sunflower oil
1 onion, peeled and chopped
1 orange pepper, deseeded
  and chopped
175 g/6 oz long-grain rice
150 ml/¼ pint orange juice
2 tbsp lemon juice
225 ml/8 fl oz vegetable stock
spray of oil
4 x 175 g/6 oz plaice fillets, skinned
1 orange
1 lemon
25 g/1 oz half-fat butter or
  low fat spread
2 tbsp freshly chopped tarragon
salt and freshly ground black pepper
lemon wedges, to garnish

TASTY TIP

Plaice is caught mainly from the North Sea and Icelandic waters. It can be bought, fresh or frozen, whole or in fillets and can be fried, poached or grilled. Dover or Lemon Sole or halibut can be used instead but they are more expensive to buy.

1 Heat the oil in a large frying pan, then sauté the onion, pepper and rice for 2 minutes.

2 Add the orange and lemon juice and bring to the boil. Reduce the heat, add half the stock and simmer for 15–20 minutes, or until the rice is tender, adding the remaining stock as necessary.

3 Preheat the grill. Finely spray the base of the grill pan with oil. Place the plaice fillets in the base and reserve.

4 Finely grate the orange and lemon rind. Squeeze the juice from half of each fruit.

5 Melt the butter or low-fat spread in a small saucepan. Add the grated rind, juice and half of the tarragon and use to baste the plaice fillets.

6 Cook one side only of the fish under the preheated grill at a medium heat for 4–6 minutes, basting continuously.

7 Once the rice is cooked, stir in the remaining tarragon and season to taste with salt and pepper. Garnish the fish with the lemon wedges and serve immediately with the rice.

2

4

5

Fish Lasagne

INGREDIENTS

Serves 4

75 g/3 oz mushrooms

1 tsp sunflower oil

1 small onion, peeled and
   finely chopped

1 tbsp freshly chopped oregano

400 g can chopped tomatoes

1 tbsp tomato purée

salt and freshly ground black pepper

450 g/1 lb cod or haddock
   fillets, skinned

9–12 sheets pre-cooked lasagne verde

For the topping:

1 medium egg, beaten

125 g/4 oz cottage cheese

150 ml/¼ pint low-fat
   natural yogurt

50 g/2 oz half-fat Cheddar
   cheese, grated

To serve:

mixed salad leaves

cherry tomatoes

1 Preheat the oven to 190°C/375°F/Gas Mark 5. Wipe the mushrooms, trim the stalks and chop. Heat the oil in a large heavy-based pan, add the onion and gently cook the onion for 3–5 minutes or until soft.

2 Stir in the mushrooms, the oregano and the chopped tomatoes with their juice.

3 Blend the tomato purée with 1 tablespoon of water. Stir into the pan and season to taste with salt and pepper.

4 Bring the sauce to the boil, then simmer uncovered for 5–10 minutes.

5 Remove as many of the tiny pin bones as possible from the fish and cut into cubes and add to the tomato sauce mixture. Stir gently and remove the pan from the heat.

6 Cover the base of an ovenproof dish with 2–3 sheets of the lasagne verde. Top with half of the fish mixture. Repeat the layers finishing with the lasagne sheets.

7 To make the topping, mix together the beaten egg, cottage cheese and yogurt. Pour over the lasagne and sprinkle with the cheese.

8 Cook the lasagne in the preheated oven for 40–45 minutes or until the topping is golden brown and bubbling. Serve the lasagne immediately with the mixed salad leaves and cherry tomatoes.

5

6

7

Fruits de Mer Stir Fry

INGREDIENTS

Serves 4

450 g/1 lb mixed fresh shellfish, such
  as tiger prawns, squid, scallops
  and mussels

2.5 cm/1 inch piece fresh root ginger

2 garlic cloves, peeled and crushed

2 green chillies, deseeded and
  finely chopped

3 tbsp light soy sauce

2 tbsp olive oil

200 g/7 oz baby sweetcorn, rinsed

200 g/7 oz asparagus tips, trimmed
  and cut in half

200 g/7 oz mangetout, trimmed

2 tbsp plum sauce

4 spring onions, trimmed
  and shredded, to garnish

freshly cooked rice, to serve

HELPFUL HINT

When stir-frying, it is important
that the wok is heated before the
oil is added. This ensures that
that the food does not stick to
the wok.

1 Prepare the shellfish. Peel the prawns and if necessary remove the thin black veins from the back of the prawns. Lightly rinse the squid rings and clean the scallops if necessary.

2 Remove and discard any mussels that are open. Scrub and debeard the remaining mussels, removing any barnacles from the shells. Cover the mussels with cold water until required.

3 Peel the root ginger and either coarsely grate or shred finely with a sharp knife and place into a small bowl.

4 Add the garlic and chillies to the small bowl, pour in the soy sauce and mix well.

5 Place the mixed shellfish, except the mussels in a bowl and pour over the marinade. Stir, cover and leave for 15 minutes.

6 Heat a wok until hot, then add the oil and heat until almost smoking. Add the prepared vegetables, stir-fry for 3 minutes, then stir in the plum sauce.

7 Add the shellfish and the mussels with the marinade and stir-fry for a further 3–4 minutes, or until the fish is cooked. Discard any mussels that have not opened. Garnish with the spring onions and serve immediately with the freshly cooked rice.

1

4

7

Zesty Whole-baked Fish

INGREDIENTS

Serves 8

1.8 kg/4 lb whole salmon, cleaned
sea salt and freshly ground
   black pepper
50 g/2 oz low-fat spread
1 garlic clove, peeled and finely sliced
zest and juice of 1 lemon
zest of 1 orange
1 tsp freshly grated nutmeg
3 tbsp Dijon mustard
2 tbsp fresh white breadcrumbs
2 bunches fresh dill
1 bunch fresh tarragon
1 lime sliced
150 ml/¼ pint half-fat
   crème fraîche
450 ml/¾ pint fromage frais
dill sprigs, to garnish

FOOD FACT

Wild salmon are normally caught in the fresh waters of North America and Northern Europe. There are many varieties: humpback (pink salmon), Chinook and sockeye. Now that they are farmed, they are more affordable.

1 Preheat the oven to 220°C/425°F/Gas Mark 7. Lightly rinse the fish and pat dry with absorbent kitchen paper. Season the cavity with a little salt and pepper. Make several diagonal cuts across the flesh of the fish and season.

2 Mix together the low-fat spread, garlic, lemon and orange zest and juice, nutmeg, mustard and fresh breadcrumbs. Mix well together. Spoon the breadcrumb mixture into the slits with a small sprig of dill. Place the remaining herbs inside the fish cavity. Weigh the fish and calculate the cooking time. Allow 10 minutes per 450 g/1 lb.

3 Lay the fish on a piece of double thickness tinfoil. If liked, smear the fish with a little low fat spread. Top with the lime slices and fold the foil into a parcel. Chill in the refrigerator for about 15 minutes.

4 Place in a roasting tin and cook in the preheated oven for the calculated cooking time. Fifteen minutes before the end of cooking, open the foil and return until the skin begins to crisp. Remove the fish from the oven and stand for 10 minutes.

5 Pour the juices from the roasting tin into a saucepan. Bring to the boil and stir in the crème fraîche and fromage frais. Simmer for 3 minutes or until hot. Garnish with dill sprigs and serve immediately.

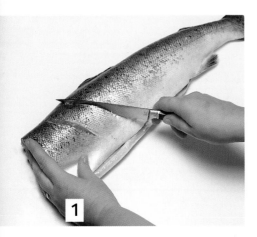

1

2

5

Seared Scallop Salad

INGREDIENTS

Serves 4

12 king (large) scallops
1 tbsp low-fat spread or butter
2 tbsp orange juice
2 tbsp balsamic vinegar
1 tbsp clear honey
2 ripe pears, washed
125 g/4 oz rocket
125 g/4 oz watercress
50 g/2 oz walnuts
freshly ground black pepper

FOOD FACT

As well as the king scallops which are used in this recipe, there are also the smaller queen scallops. It is worth noting that scallops are in season between September and March, when they will not only be at their best, but they may also be slightly cheaper in price. When buying, especially the larger king scallop, make sure that the orange roe is left intact.

1 Clean the scallops removing the thin black vein from around the white meat and coral. Rinse thoroughly and dry on absorbent kitchen paper.

2 Cut into 2–3 thick slices, depending on the scallop size.

3 Heat a griddle pan or heavy-based frying pan, then when hot, add the low-fat spread or butter and allow to melt.

4 Once melted, sear the scallops for 1 minute on each side or until golden. Remove from the pan and reserve.

5 Briskly whisk together the orange juice, balsamic vinegar and honey to make the dressing and reserve.

6 With a small, sharp knife carefully cut the pears into quarters, core then cut into chunks.

7 Mix the rocket leaves, watercress, pear chunks and walnuts. Pile on to serving plates and top with the scallops.

8 Drizzle over the dressing and grind over plenty of black pepper. Serve immediately.

1

4

6

Fish Roulades with Rice & Spinach

INGREDIENTS

Serves 4

4 x 175 g/6 oz lemon sole, skinned
salt and freshly ground black pepper
1 tsp fennel seeds
75 g/3 oz long-grain rice, cooked
150 g/5 oz white crab meat, fresh
    or canned
125 g/4 oz baby spinach, washed
    and trimmed
5 tbsp dry white wine
5 tbsp half-fat crème fraîche
2 tbsp freshly chopped parsley, plus
    extra to garnish
asparagus spears, to serve

1 Wipe each fish fillet with either a clean damp cloth or kitchen paper. Place on a chopping board, skinned side up and season lightly with salt and black pepper.

2 Place the fennel seeds in a pestle and mortar and crush lightly. Transfer to a small bowl and stir in the cooked rice. Drain the crab meat thoroughly. Add to the rice mixture and mix lightly.

3 Lay 2–3 spinach leaves over each fillet and top with a quarter of the crab meat mixture. Roll up and secure with a cocktail stick if necessary. Place into a large pan and pour over the wine. Cover and cook on a medium heat for 5–7 minutes or until cooked.

4 Remove the fish from the cooking liquor, and transfer to a serving plate and keep warm. Stir the crème fraîche into the cooking liquor and season to taste. Heat for 3 minutes, then stir in the chopped parsley.

5 Spoon the sauce on to the base of a plate. Cut each roulade into slices and arrange on top of the sauce. Serve with freshly cooked asparagus spears.

FOOD FACT

Spinach is one of the healthiest, leafy green vegetables to be eaten. It also acts as an antioxidant and it is suggested that it can reduce risks of certain cancers. Why not use whole-grain rice to add nutritional value and to give the dish a nuttier taste.

2

3

4

Chicken with Roasted Fennel & Citrus Rice

INGREDIENTS

Serves 4

2 tsp fennel seeds
1 tbsp freshly chopped oregano
1 garlic clove, peeled and crushed
salt and freshly ground black pepper
4 chicken quarters, about
   175 g/6 oz each
½ lemon, finely sliced
1 fennel bulb, trimmed
2 tsp olive oil
4 plum tomatoes
25 g/1 oz stoned green olives

To garnish:
fennel fronds,
orange slices

Citrus rice:
225 g/8 oz long-grain rice
finely grated rind and juice
   of ½ lemon
150 ml/¼ pint orange juice
450 ml/¾ pint boiling chicken or
   vegetable stock

1 Preheat the oven to 200°C/400°F/Gas Mark 6. Lightly crush the fennel seeds and mix with the oregano, garlic, salt and pepper. Place between the skin and flesh of the chicken breasts, careful not to tear the skin. Arrange the lemon slices on top of the chicken.

2 Cut the fennel into 8 wedges. Place on a baking tray with the chicken. Lightly brush the fennel with the oil. Cook the chicken and fennel on the top shelf of the preheated oven for 10 minutes.

3 Meanwhile, put the rice in a 2.3 litre/4 pint ovenproof dish. Stir in the lemon rind and juice, orange juice and stock. Cover with a lid and put on the middle shelf of the oven.

4 Reduce the oven temperature to 180°C/350°F/Gas Mark 4. Cook the chicken for a further 40 minutes, turning the fennel wedges and lemon slices once. Deseed and chop the tomatoes. Add to the tray and cook for 5–10 minutes. Remove from the oven.

5 When cooled slightly, remove the chicken skin and discard. Fluff the rice, and scatter the olives over the dish. Garnish with fennel fronds, orange slices and serve.

1

3

4

Braised Chicken in Beer

INGREDIENTS

Serves 4

4 chicken joints, skinned
125 g/4 oz pitted dried prunes
2 bay leaves
12 shallots
2 tsp olive oil
125 g/4 oz small button
  mushrooms, wiped
1 tsp soft dark brown sugar
½ tsp whole-grain mustard
2 tsp tomato purée
150 ml/¼ pint light ale
150 ml/¼ pint chicken stock
salt and freshly ground black pepper
2 tsp cornflour
2 tsp lemon juice
2 tbsp chopped fresh parsley
flat-leaf parsley, to garnish

To serve:
mashed potatoes
seasonal green vegetables

1. Preheat the oven to 170°C/325°F/Gas Mark 3. Cut each chicken joint in half and put in an ovenproof casserole dish with the prunes and bay leaves.

2. To peel the shallots, put in a small bowl and cover with boiling water.

3. Drain the shallots after 2 minutes and rinse under cold water until cool enough to handle. The skins should then peel away easily from the shallots.

4. Heat the oil in a large non-stick frying pan. Add the shallots and gently cook for about 5 minutes until beginning to colour.

5. Add the mushrooms to the pan and cook for a further 3–4 minutes until both the mushrooms and onions are softened.

6. Sprinkle the sugar over the shallots and mushrooms, then add the mustard, tomato purée, ale and chicken stock. Season to taste with salt and pepper and bring to the boil, stirring to combine. Carefully pour over the chicken.

7. Cover the casserole and cook in the preheated oven for 1 hour. Blend the cornflour with the lemon juice and 1 tablespoon of cold water and stir into the chicken casserole.

8. Return the casserole to the oven for a further 10 minutes or until the chicken is cooked and the vegetables are tender.

9. Remove the bay leaves and stir in the chopped parsley. Garnish the chicken with the flat-leaf parsley. Serve with the mashed potatoes and fresh green vegetables.

Chicken Baked in a Salt Crust

INGREDIENTS

Serves 4

1.8 kg/4 lb oven-ready chicken
salt and freshly ground black pepper
1 medium onion, peeled
sprig of fresh rosemary
sprig of fresh thyme
1 bay leaf
15 g/½ oz butter, softened
1 garlic clove, peeled and crushed
pinch of ground paprika
finely grated rind of ½ lemon

To garnish:
fresh herbs
lemon slices

Salt crust:
900 g/2 lb plain flour
450 g/1 lb fine cooking salt
450 g/1 lb coarse sea salt
2 tbsp oil

HELPFUL HINT

It is best to avoid eating the skin
from the chicken. It is high in fat
and also absorbs a lot of salt from
the crust.

1 Preheat the oven to 170°C/325°F/Gas Mark 3. Remove the giblets if
necessary and rinse the chicken with cold water. Sprinkle the inside
with salt and pepper. Put the onion inside with the rosemary, thyme
and bay leaf.

2 Mix the butter, garlic, paprika and lemon rind together. Starting at
the neck end, gently ease the skin from the chicken and push the
mixture under.

3 To make the salt crust, put the flour and salts in a large mixing bowl
and stir together. Make a well in the centre. Pour in 600 ml/1 pint of
cold water and the oil. Mix to a stiff dough, then knead on a lightly
floured surface for 2–3 minutes. Roll out the pastry to a circle with a
diameter of about 51 cm/20 inches. Place the chicken breast side
down in the middle. Lightly brush the edges with water, then fold
over to enclose. Pinch the joints together to seal.

4 Put the chicken join side down in a roasting tin and cook in the
preheated oven for 2¾ hours. Remove from the oven and stand
for 20 minutes.

5 Break open the hard crust and remove the chicken. Discard the
crust. Remove the skin from the chicken, garnish with the fresh
herbs and lemon slices. Serve the chicken immediately.

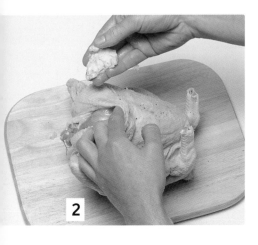

2

3

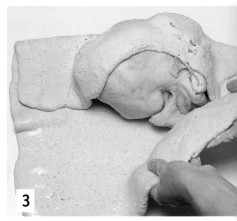

3

Spicy Chicken Skewers with Mango Tabbouleh

INGREDIENTS

Serves 4

400 g/14 oz chicken breast fillets
200 ml/7 fl oz natural low fat yogurt
1 garlic clove, peeled and crushed
1 small red chilli, deseeded
  and finely chopped
½ tsp ground turmeric
finely grated rind and juice
  of ½ lemon
sprigs of fresh mint, to garnish

Mango tabbouleh:

175 g/6 oz bulgur wheat
1 tsp olive oil
juice of ½ lemon
½ red onion, finely chopped
1 ripe mango, halved, stoned, peeled
  and chopped
¼ cucumber, finely diced
2 tbsp freshly chopped parsley
2 tbsp freshly shredded mint
salt and finely ground black pepper

1. If using wooden skewers, pre-soak them in cold water for at least 30 minutes. (This stops them from burning during grilling.)

2. Cut the chicken into 5 x 1 cm/2 x ½ inch strips and place in a shallow dish.

3. Mix together the yogurt, garlic, chilli, turmeric, lemon rind and juice. Pour over the chicken and toss to coat. Cover and leave to marinate in the refrigerator for up to 8 hours.

4. To make the tabbouleh, put the bulgur wheat in a bowl. Pour over enough boiling water to cover. Put a plate over the bowl. Leave to soak for 20 minutes.

5. Whisk together the oil and lemon juice in a bowl. Add the red onion and leave to marinade for 10 minutes.

6. Drain the bulgur wheat and squeeze out any excess moisture in a clean tea towel. Add to the red onion with the mango, cucumber, herbs and season to taste with salt and pepper. Toss together.

7. Thread the chicken strips on to 8 wooden or metal skewers. Cook under a hot grill for 8 minutes. Turn and brush with the marinade, until the chicken is lightly browned and cooked through.

8. Spoon the tabbouleh on to individual plates. Arrange the chicken skewers on top and garnish with the sprigs of mint. Serve warm or cold.

3

4

6

Pan-cooked Chicken with Thai Spices

INGREDIENTS

Serves 4

4 kaffir lime leaves

5 cm/2 inch piece of root ginger,
   peeled and chopped

300 ml/½ pint chicken
   stock, boiling

4 x 175 g/6 oz chicken breasts

2 tsp groundnut oil

5 tbsp coconut milk

1 tbsp fish sauce

2 red chillies, deseeded
   and finely chopped

225 g/8 oz Thai jasmine rice

1 tbsp lime juice

3 tbsp freshly chopped coriander

salt and freshly ground black pepper

To garnish:

wedges of lime

freshly chopped coriander

FOOD FACT

Fresh kaffir lime leaves can be found in Oriental food stores. Most supermarkets now stock dried kaffir lime leaves. If using dried, crumble lightly and use as above.

1 Lightly bruise the kaffir lime leaves and put in a bowl with the chopped ginger. Pour over the chicken stock, cover and leave to infuse for 30 minutes.

2 Meanwhile, cut each chicken breast into two pieces. Heat the oil in a large, non-stick frying pan or flameproof casserole dish and brown the chicken pieces for 2–3 minutes on each side.

3 Strain the infused chicken stock into the pan. Half cover the pan with a lid and gently simmer for 10 minutes.

4 Stir in the coconut milk, fish sauce and chopped chillies. Simmer, uncovered for 5–6 minutes, or until the chicken is tender and cooked through and the sauce has reduced slightly.

5 Meanwhile, cook the rice in boiling salted water according to the packet instructions. Drain the rice thoroughly.

6 Stir the lime juice and chopped coriander into the sauce. Season to taste with salt and pepper. Serve the chicken and sauce on a bed of rice. Garnish with wedges of lime and freshly chopped coriander and serve immediately.

Sauvignon Chicken & Mushroom Filo Pie

INGREDIENTS

Serves 4

1 onion, peeled and chopped
1 leek, trimmed and chopped
225 ml/8 fl oz chicken stock
3 x 175 g/6 oz chicken breasts
150 ml/¼ pint dry white wine
1 bay leaf
175 g/6 oz baby button mushrooms
2 tbsp plain flour
1 tbsp freshly chopped tarragon
salt and freshly ground black pepper
sprig of fresh parsley, to garnish
seasonal vegetables, to serve

Topping:

75 g/3 oz (about 5 sheets) filo pastry
1 tbsp sunflower oil
1 tsp sesame seeds

1 Preheat the oven to 190°C/375°F/Gas Mark 5. Put the onion and leek in a heavy-based saucepan with 125 ml/4 fl oz of the stock.

2 Bring to the boil, cover and simmer for 5 minutes, then uncover and cook until all the stock has evaporated and the vegetables are tender.

3 Cut the chicken into bite-sized cubes. Add to the pan with the remaining stock, wine and bay leaf. Cover and gently simmer for 5 minutes. Add the mushrooms and simmer for a further 5 minutes.

4 Blend the flour with 3 tablespoons of cold water. Stir into the pan and cook, stirring all the time until the sauce has thickened.

5 Stir the tarragon into the sauce and season with salt and pepper.

6 Spoon the mixture into a 1.2 litre/2 pint pie dish, discarding the bay leaf.

7 Lightly brush a sheet of filo pastry with a little of the oil.

8 Crumple the pastry slightly. Arrange on top of the filling. Repeat with the remaining filo sheets and oil, then sprinkle the top of the pie with the sesame seeds.

9 Bake the pie on the middle shelf of the preheated oven for 20 minutes until the filo pastry topping is golden and crisp. Garnish with a sprig of parsley. Serve the pie immediately with the seasonal vegetables.

3

6

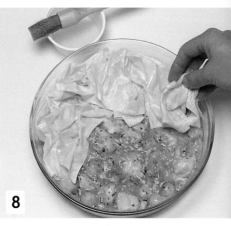

8

Chilli Roast Chicken

INGREDIENTS

Serves 4

3 medium-hot fresh red
  chillies, deseeded

½ tsp ground turmeric

1 tsp cumin seeds

1 tsp coriander seeds

2 garlic cloves, peeled and crushed

2.5 cm/1 inch piece fresh root ginger,
  peeled and chopped

1 tbsp lemon juice

1 tbsp olive oil

2 tbsp roughly chopped
  fresh coriander

½ tsp salt

freshly ground black pepper

1.4 kg/3 lb oven-ready chicken

15 g/½ oz unsalted butter, melted

550 g/1¼ lb butternut squash

fresh parsley and coriander sprigs,
  to garnish

To serve:

4 baked potatoes

seasonal green vegetables

1 Preheat the oven to 190°C/375°F/Gas Mark 5. Roughly chop the chillies and put in a food processor with the turmeric, cumin seeds, coriander seeds, garlic, ginger, lemon juice, olive oil, coriander, salt, pepper and 2 tablespoons of cold water. Blend to a paste, leaving the ingredients still slightly chunky.

2 Starting at the neck end of the chicken, gently ease up the skin to loosen it from the breast. Reserve 3 tablespoons of the paste. Push the remaining paste over the chicken breast under the skin, spreading it evenly.

3 Put the chicken in a large roasting tin. Mix the reserved chilli paste with the melted butter. Use 1 tablespoon to brush evenly over the chicken, roast in the preheated oven for 20 minutes.

4 Meanwhile, halve, peel and scoop out the seeds from the butternut squash. Cut into large chunks and mix in the remaining chilli paste and butter mixture.

5 Arrange the butternut squash around the chicken. Roast for a further hour, basting with the cooking juices about every 20 minutes until the chicken is fully cooked and the squash tender. Garnish with parsley and coriander. Serve hot with baked potatoes and green vegetables.

1

2

4

Aromatic Chicken Curry

INGREDIENTS

Serves 4

125 g/4 oz red lentils
2 tsp ground coriander
½ tsp cumin seeds
2 tsp mild curry paste
1 bay leaf
small strip of lemon rind
600 ml/1 pint chicken or
    vegetable stock
8 chicken thighs, skinned
175 g/6 oz spinach leaves, rinsed
    and shredded
1 tbsp freshly chopped coriander
2 tsp lemon juice
salt and freshly ground black pepper

To serve:
freshly cooked rice
low fat natural yogurt

HELPFUL HINT

Dry-frying spices releases their flavour and is a technique that can be used in many dishes. Try mixing dry-fried spices with a little water or oil to make a paste. Spread the paste on meat or fish before baking to make a spicy crust.

1 Put the lentils in a sieve and rinse thoroughly under cold running water.

2 Dry-fry the ground coriander and cumin seeds in a large saucepan over a low heat for about 30 seconds. Stir in the curry paste.

3 Add the lentils to the saucepan with the bay leaf and lemon rind, then pour in the stock.

4 Stir, then slowly bring to the boil. Turn down the heat, half-cover the pan with a lid and simmer gently for 5 minutes, stirring occasionally.

5 Secure the chicken thighs with cocktail sticks to keep their shape. Place in the pan and half-cover. Simmer for 15 minutes.

6 Stir in the shredded spinach and cook for a further 25 minutes or until the chicken is very tender and the sauce is thick.

7 Remove the bay leaf and lemon rind. Stir in the coriander and lemon juice, then season to taste with salt and pepper. Serve immediately with the rice and a little natural yogurt.

3

5

6

Cheesy Chicken Burgers

INGREDIENTS

Serves 6

1 tbsp sunflower oil
1 small onion, peeled and
   finely chopped
1 garlic clove, peeled and crushed
½ red pepper, deseeded and
   finely chopped
450 g/1 lb fresh chicken mince
2 tbsp 0%-fat Greek yogurt
50 g/2 oz fresh brown breadcrumbs
1 tbsp freshly chopped herbs, such as
   parsley or tarragon
50 g/2 oz Cheshire cheese, crumbled
salt and freshly ground black pepper

For the sweetcorn and carrot relish:

200 g can sweetcorn, drained
1 carrot, peeled, grated
½ green chilli, deseeded and
   finely chopped
2 tsp cider vinegar
2 tsp light soft brown sugar

To serve:

wholemeal or granary rolls
lettuce
sliced tomatoes
mixed salad leaves

1 Preheat the grill. Heat the oil in a frying pan and gently cook the onion and garlic for 5 minutes. Add the red pepper and cook for 5 minutes. Transfer into a mixing bowl and reserve.

2 Add the chicken, yogurt, breadcrumbs, herbs and cheese and season to taste with salt and pepper. Mix well.

3 Divide the mixture equally into 6 and shape into burgers. Cover and chill in the refrigerator for at least 20 minutes.

4 To make the relish, put all the ingredients in a small saucepan with 1 tablespoon of water and heat gently, stirring occasionally until all the sugar has dissolved.

5 Cover and cook over a low heat for 2 minutes, then uncover and cook for a further minute, or until the relish is thick.

6 Place the burgers on a lightly oiled grill pan and grill under a medium heat for 8–10 minutes on each side, or until browned and completely cooked through.

7 Warm the rolls if liked, then split in half and fill with the burgers, lettuce, sliced tomatoes and the prepared relish. Serve immediately with the salad leaves.

2

4

6

Chicken Cacciatore

INGREDIENTS

Serves 4

4 chicken leg portions
1 tbsp olive oil
1 red onion, peeled and cut into very
   thin wedges
1 garlic clove, peeled and crushed
sprig of fresh thyme
sprig of fresh rosemary
150 ml/¼ pint dry white wine
200 ml/7 fl oz chicken stock
400 g can chopped tomatoes
40 g/1½ oz black olives, pitted
15 g/½ oz capers, drained
salt and freshly ground black pepper
freshly cooked fettuccine, linguine or
   pasta shells

HELPFUL HINT

When watching your saturated fat intake, it is essential to remove the skin from the chicken before eating. Any fat is deposited directly underneath the skin.

1. Skin the chicken portions and cut each one into 2 pieces to make 4 thighs and 4 drumsticks.

2. Heat 2 teaspoons of the oil in a flameproof casserole dish and cook the chicken for 2–3 minutes on each side until lightly browned. Remove the chicken from the pan and reserve.

3. Add the remaining 1 teaspoon of oil to the juices in the pan.

4. Add the red onion and gently cook for 5 minutes, stirring occasionally.

5. Add the garlic and cook for a further 5 minutes until soft and beginning to brown. Return the chicken to the pan.

6. Add the herbs, then pour in the wine and let it bubble for 1–2 minutes.

7. Add the stock and tomatoes, cover and gently simmer for 15 minutes.

8. Stir in the olives and capers. Cook uncovered for a further 5 minutes or until the chicken is cooked and the sauce thickened. Remove the herbs and season to taste with salt and pepper.

9. Place the chicken on a bed of pasta, allowing one thigh and one drumstick per person. Spoon over the sauce and serve.

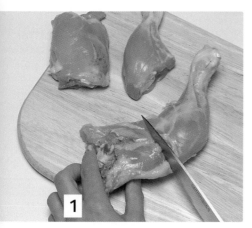

Chicken & Summer Vegetable Risotto

INGREDIENTS

Serves 4

1 litre/1¾ pint chicken or
  vegetable stock
225 g/8 oz baby asparagus spears
125 g/4 oz French beans
15 g/½ oz butter
1 small onion, peeled and
  finely chopped
150 ml/¼ pint dry white wine
275 g/10 oz arborio rice
pinch of saffron strands
75 g/3 oz frozen peas, thawed
225 g/8 oz cooked chicken, skinned
  and diced
juice of ½ lemon
salt and freshly ground black pepper
25 g/1 oz Parmesan, shaved

1 Bring the stock to the boil in a large saucepan. Trim the asparagus and cut into 4 cm/1½ inch lengths.

2 Blanch the asparagus in the stock for 1–2 minutes or until tender, then remove with a slotted spoon and reserve.

3 Halve the green beans and cook in the boiling stock for 4 minutes. Remove and reserve. Turn down the heat and keep the stock barely simmering.

4 Melt the butter in a heavy-based saucepan. Add the onion and cook gently for about 5 minutes.

5 Pour the wine into the pan and boil rapidly until the liquid has almost reduced. Add the rice and cook, stirring for 1 minute until the grains are coated and look translucent.

6 Add the saffron and a ladle of the stock. Simmer, stirring all the time, until the stock has absorbed. Continue adding the stock, a ladle at a time, until it has all been absorbed.

7 After 15 minutes the risotto should be creamy with a slight bite to it. If not add a little more stock and cook for a few more minutes, or until it is of the correct texture and consistency.

8 Add the peas, reserved vegetables, chicken and lemon juice. Season to taste with salt and pepper and cook for 3-4 minutes or until the chicken is thoroughly heated and piping hot.

9 Spoon the risotto on to warmed serving plates. Scatter each portion with a few shavings of Parmesan cheese and serve immediately.

2

5

6

Mexican Chicken

INGREDIENTS

Serves 4

1.4 kg/3 lb oven-ready
   chicken, jointed
3 tbsp plain flour
½ tsp ground paprika pepper
salt and freshly ground black pepper
2 tsp sunflower oil
1 small onion, peeled and chopped
1 red chilli, deseeded and
   finely chopped
½ tsp ground cumin
½ tsp dried oregano
300 ml/½ pint chicken or
   vegetable stock
1 green pepper, deseeded
   and sliced
2 tsp cocoa powder
1 tbsp lime juice
2 tsp clear honey
3 tbsp 0%-fat Greek yogurt

To garnish:
sliced limes
red chilli slices
sprig of fresh oregano

To serve:
freshly cooked rice
fresh green salad leaves

1 Using a knife, remove the skin from the chicken joints.

2 In a shallow dish, mix together the flour, paprika, salt and pepper. Coat the chicken on both sides with flour and shake off any excess if necessary.

3 Heat the oil in a large non-stick frying pan. Add the chicken and brown on both sides. Transfer to a plate and reserve.

4 Add the onion and red chilli to the pan and gently cook for 5 minutes, or until the onion is soft. Stir occasionally.

5 Stir in the cumin and oregano and cook for a further minute. Pour in the stock and bring to the boil.

6 Return the chicken to the pan, cover and cook for 40 minutes. Add the green pepper and cook for 10 minutes, until the chicken is cooked. Remove the chicken and pepper with a slotted spoon and keep warm in a serving dish.

7 Blend the cocoa powder with 1 tablespoon of warm water. Stir into the sauce, then boil rapidly until the sauce has thickened and reduced by about one third. Stir in the lime juice, honey and yogurt.

8 Pour the sauce over the chicken and pepper and garnish with the lime slices, chilli and oregano. Serve immediately with the freshly cooked rice and green salad.

2

5

7

Turkey & Tomato Tagine

INGREDIENTS

Serves 4

Meatballs:

450 g/1 lb fresh turkey mince
1 small onion, peeled and very
   finely chopped
1 garlic clove, peeled and crushed
1 tbsp freshly chopped coriander
1 tsp ground cumin
1 tbsp olive oil
salt and freshly ground black pepper

Sauce:

1 onion, peeled and finely chopped
1 garlic clove, peeled and crushed
150 ml/¼ pint turkey stock
400 g can chopped tomatoes
½ tsp ground cumin
½ tsp ground cinnamon
pinch of cayenne pepper
freshly chopped parsley
freshly chopped herbs, to garnish
freshly cooked couscous or rice,
   to serve

1 Preheat the oven to 190°C/375°F/Gas Mark 5. Put all the ingredients for the meatballs in a bowl, except the oil and mix well. Season to taste with salt and pepper. Shape into 20 balls, about the size of walnuts.

2 Put on a tray, cover lightly and chill in the refrigerator while making the sauce.

3 Put the onion and garlic in a pan with 125 ml/4 fl oz of the stock. Cook over a low heat until all the stock has evaporated. Continue cooking for 1 minute, or until the onions begin to colour.

4 Add the remaining stock to the pan with the tomatoes, cumin, cinnamon and cayenne pepper. Simmer for 10 minutes, until slightly thickened and reduced. Stir in the parsley and season to taste.

5 Heat the oil in a large non-stick frying pan and cook the meatballs in two batches until lightly browned all over.

6 Lift the meatballs out with a slotted spoon and drain on kitchen paper.

7 Pour the sauce into a tagine or an ovenproof casserole dish . Top with the meatballs, cover and cook in the preheated oven for 25–30 minutes, or until the meatballs are cooked through and the sauce is bubbling. Garnish with freshly chopped herbs and serve immediately on a bed of couscous or plain boiled rice.

1

4

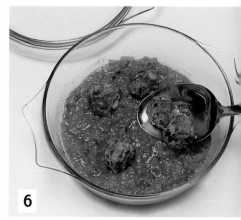

6

Turkey Escalopes with Apricot Chutney

INGREDIENTS

Serves 4

4 x 175–225 g/6–8 oz turkey steaks
1 tbsp plain flour
salt and freshly ground black pepper
1 tbsp olive oil
flat-leaf parsley sprigs, to garnish
orange wedges, to serve

Apricot chutney:

125 g/4 oz no-need-to-soak dried
  apricots, chopped
1 red onion, peeled and
  finely chopped
1 tsp grated fresh root ginger
2 tbsp caster sugar
finely grated rind of ½ orange
125 ml/4 fl oz fresh orange juice
125 ml/4 fl oz ruby port
1 whole clove

1   Put a turkey steak on to a sheet of non-pvc clingfilm or non-stick baking parchment. Cover with a second sheet.

2   Using a rolling pin, gently pound the turkey until the meat is flattened to about 5 mm/¼ inch thick. Repeat to make 4 escalopes.

3   Mix the flour with the salt and pepper and use to lightly dust the turkey escalopes.

4   Put the turkey escalopes on a board or baking tray and cover with a piece of non-pvc clingfilm or non-stick baking parchment. Chill in the refrigerator until ready to cook.

5   For the apricot chutney, put the apricots, onion, ginger, sugar, orange rind, orange juice, port and clove into a saucepan.

6   Slowly bring to the boil and simmer, uncovered for 10 minutes, stirring occasionally, until thick and syrupy.

7   Remove the clove and stir in the chopped coriander.

8   Heat the oil in a pan and chargriddle the turkey escalopes, in two batches if necessary, for 3–4 minutes on each side until golden brown and tender.

9   Spoon the chutney on to four individual serving plates. Place a turkey escalope on top of each spoonful of chutney. Garnish with sprigs of parsley and serve immediately with orange wedges.

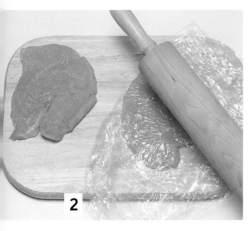

2

5

8

Smoked Turkey Tagliatelle

INGREDIENTS

Serves 4

2 tsp olive oil

1 bunch spring onions, trimmed and
  diagonally sliced

1 garlic clove, peeled and crushed

1 small courgette, trimmed, sliced
  and cut in half

4 tbsp dry white wine

400 g can chopped tomatoes

2 tbsp freshly shredded basil

salt and freshly ground black pepper

225 g/8 oz spinach and egg tagliatelle

225 g/8 oz smoked turkey breast, cut
  into strips

small fresh basil leaves, to garnish

TASTY TIP

Many shops and supermarkets
now stock flavoured pasta as well
as the plain traditional type. Why
not try using a garlic and herb
or sundried tomato tagliatelle in
this recipe.

1 Heat the oil in a saucepan. Add the spring onions and garlic and gently cook for 2–3 minutes, until beginning to soften. Stir in the sliced courgette and cook for 1 minute.

2 Add the wine and let it bubble for 1–2 minutes. Stir in the chopped tomatoes, bring to the boil and simmer uncovered over a low heat for 15 minutes, or until the courgettes are tender and the sauce slightly reduced. Stir the shredded basil into the sauce and season to taste with salt and pepper.

3 Meanwhile, bring a large pan of salted water to the boil. Add the tagliatelle and cook for 10 minutes, until al dente or according to the packet instructions. Drain thoroughly.

4 Return the tagliatelle to the pan, add half the tomato sauce and toss together to coat the pasta thoroughly in the sauce. Cover with a lid and reserve.

5 Add the strips of turkey to the remaining sauce and heat gently for 2–3 minutes until piping hot.

6 Divide the tagliatelle among four serving plates. Spoon over the sauce, garnish with basil leaves and serve immediately.

1

2

5

Turkey & Mixed Mushroom Lasagne

INGREDIENTS

Serves 4

1 tbsp olive oil

225 g/8 oz mixed mushrooms e.g.
button, chestnut and portabello,
wiped and sliced

15 g/½ oz butter

25 g/1 oz plain flour

300 ml/½ pint skimmed milk

1 bay leaf

225 g/8 oz cooked turkey, cubed

¼ tsp freshly grated nutmeg

salt and freshly ground black pepper

400 g can plum tomatoes, drained
and chopped

1 tsp dried mixed herbs

9 lasagne sheets (about 150 g/5 oz)

For the topping:

200 ml/7 fl oz 0%-fat Greek yogurt

1 medium egg, lightly beaten

1 tbsp finely grated Parmesan cheese

mixed salad leaves, to serve

1 Preheat the oven to 180°C/350°F/Gas Mark 4. Heat the oil and cook the mushrooms until tender and all the juices have evaporated. Remove and reserve.

2 Put the butter, flour, milk and bay leaf in the pan. Slowly bring to the boil, stirring until thickened. Simmer for 2–3 minutes. Remove the bay leaf and stir in the mushrooms, turkey, nutmeg, salt and pepper.

3 Mix together the tomatoes, mixed herbs and season with salt and pepper. Spoon half into the base of a 1.7 litre/3 pint ovenproof dish. Top with 3 sheets of lasagne, then with half the turkey mixture. Repeat the layers, then arrange the remaining 3 sheets of pasta on top.

4 Mix together the yogurt and egg. Spoon over the lasagne, spreading the mixture into the corners. Sprinkle with the Parmesan and bake in the preheated oven for 45 minutes. Serve with the mixed salad.

2

3

4

Teriyaki Turkey with Oriental Vegetables

INGREDIENTS

Serves 4

1 red chilli
1 garlic clove, peeled and crushed
2.5 cm/1 inch piece root ginger,
  peeled and grated
3 tbsp dark soy sauce
1 tsp sunflower oil
350 g/12 oz skinless, boneless
  turkey breast
1 tbsp sesame oil
1 tbsp sesame seeds
2 carrots, peeled and cut into
  matchstick strips
1 leek, trimmed and shredded
125 g/4 oz broccoli, cut into
  tiny florets
1 tsp cornflour
3 tbsp dry sherry
125 g/4 oz mangetout, cut into
  thin strips

To serve:
freshly cooked egg noodles
sprinkling of sesame seeds

1 Halve, deseed and thinly slice the chilli. Put into a small bowl with the garlic, ginger, soy sauce and sunflower oil.

2 Cut the turkey into thin strips. Add to the mixture and mix until well coated. Cover with clingfilm and marinate in the refrigerator for at least 30 minutes.

3 Heat a wok or large frying pan. Add 2 teaspoons of the sesame oil. When hot, remove the turkey from the marinade. Stir-fry for 2–3 minutes until browned and cooked. Remove from the pan and reserve.

4 Heat the remaining 1 teaspoon of oil in the wok. Add the sesame seeds and stir-fry for a few seconds until they start to change colour.

5 Add the carrots, leek and broccoli and continue stir-frying for 2–3 minutes.

6 Blend the cornflour with 1 tablespoon of cold water to make a smooth paste. Stir in the sherry and marinade. Add to the wok with the mangetout and cook for 1 minute, stirring all the time until thickened.

7 Return the turkey to the pan and continue cooking for 1–2 minutes or until the turkey is hot, the vegetables are tender and the sauce is bubbling. Serve the turkey and vegetables immediately with the egg noodles. Sprinkle with the sesame seeds.

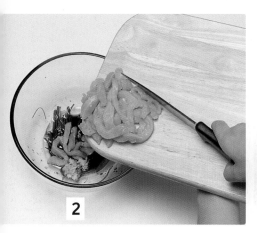

2

3

5

Guinea Fowl with Calvados & Apples

INGREDIENTS

Serves 4

4 guinea fowl supremes, each about
  150 g/5 oz, skinned
1 tbsp plain flour
1 tbsp sunflower oil
1 onion, peeled and finely sliced
1 garlic clove, peeled and crushed
1 tsp freshly chopped thyme
150 ml/¼ pint dry cider
salt and freshly ground black pepper
3 tbsp Calvados brandy
sprigs of fresh thyme, to garnish

Caramelised apples:

15 g/½ oz unsalted butter
2 red-skinned eating apples,
  quartered, cored and sliced
1 tsp caster sugar

1. Lightly dust the guinea fowl supremes with the flour.

2. Heat 2 teaspoons of the oil in a large non-stick frying pan and cook the supremes for 2–3 minutes on each side until browned. Remove from the pan and reserve.

3. Heat the remaining teaspoon of oil in the pan and add the onion and garlic. Cook over a medium heat for 10 minutes, stirring occasionally until soft and just beginning to colour.

4. Stir in the chopped thyme and cider. Return the guinea fowl to the pan, season with salt and pepper and bring to a very gentle simmer. Cover and cook over a low heat for 15–20 minutes or until the guinea fowl is tender.

5. Remove the guinea fowl and keep warm. Turn up the heat and boil the sauce until thickened and reduced by half.

6. Meanwhile, prepare the caramelised apples. Melt the butter in a small non-stick pan, add the apple slices in a single layer and sprinkle with the sugar. Cook until the apples are tender and beginning to caramelise, turning once.

7. Put the Calvados in a metal ladle or small saucepan and gently heat until warm. Carefully set alight with a match, let the flames die down, then stir into the sauce.

8. Serve the guinea fowl with the sauce spooned over and garnished with the caramelised apples and sprigs of fresh thyme.

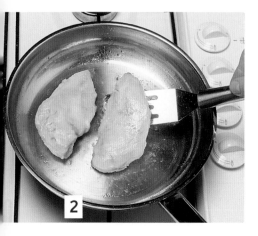

Duck with Berry Sauce

INGREDIENTS

Serves 4

4 x 175 g/6 oz boneless duck breasts
salt and freshly ground black pepper
1 tsp sunflower oil

Sauce:

juice of 1 orange
1 bay leaf
3 tbsp redcurrant jelly
150 g/5 oz fresh or frozen
   mixed berries
2 tbsp dried cranberries or cherries
$\frac{1}{2}$ tsp soft light brown sugar
1 tbsp balsamic vinegar
1 tsp freshly chopped mint
sprigs of fresh mint, to garnish

To serve:

freshly cooked potatoes
freshly cooked green beans

1 Remove the skins from the duck breasts and season with a little salt and pepper. Brush a griddle pan with the oil, then heat on the stove until smoking hot.

2 Place the duck, skinned-side down in the pan. Cook over a medium-high heat for 5 minutes, or until well browned. Turn the duck and cook for 2 minutes. Lower the heat and cook for a further 5–8 minutes, or until cooked, but still slightly pink in the centre. Remove from the pan and keep warm.

3 While the duck is cooking, make the sauce. Put the orange juice, bay leaf, redcurrant jelly, fresh or frozen and dried berries and sugar in a small griddle pan. Add any juices left in the griddle pan to the small pan. Slowly bring to the boil, lower the heat and simmer uncovered for 4–5 minutes, until the fruit is soft.

4 Remove the bay leaf. Stir in the vinegar and chopped mint and season to taste with salt and pepper.

5 Slice the duck breasts on the diagonal and arrange on serving plates. Spoon over the berry sauce and garnish with sprigs of fresh mint. Serve immediately with the potatoes and green beans.

HELPFUL HINT

Duck breasts are best served slightly pink in the middle. Whole ducks, however, should be thoroughly cooked.

Sticky–glazed Spatchcocked Poussins

INGREDIENTS

Serves 4

2 poussins, each about
  700 g/1½ lb
salt and freshly ground black pepper
4 kumquats, thinly sliced
assorted salad leaves, crusty bread or
  new potatoes, to serve

For the glaze:

zest of 1 small lemon, finely grated
1 tbsp lemon juice
1 tbsp dry sherry
2 tbsp clear honey
2 tbsp dark soy sauce
2 tbsp whole-grain mustard
1 tsp tomato purée
½ tsp Chinese five-spice powder

1 Preheat the grill just before cooking. Place one of the poussins breast-side down on a board. Using poultry shears, cut down one side of the backbone. Cut down the other side of the backbone. Remove the bone.

2 Open out the poussin and press down hard on the breast bone with the heel of your hand to break it and to flatten the poussin.

3 Thread two skewers crosswise through the bird to keep it flat, ensuring that each skewer goes through a wing and out through the leg on the opposite side. Repeat with the other bird. Season both sides of the bird with salt and pepper.

4 To make the glaze, mix together the lemon zest and juice, sherry, honey, soy sauce, mustard, tomato purée and Chinese five-spice powder and use to brush all over the poussins.

5 Place the poussins skin-side down on a grill rack and grill under a medium heat for 15 minutes, brushing halfway through with more glaze.

6 Turn the poussins over and grill for 10 minutes. Brush again with glaze and arrange the kumquat slices on top. Grill for a further 15 minutes until well-browned and cooked through. If they start to brown too quickly, turn down the grill a little.

7 Remove the skewers and cut each poussin in half along the breastbone. Serve immediately with the salad, crusty bread or new potatoes.

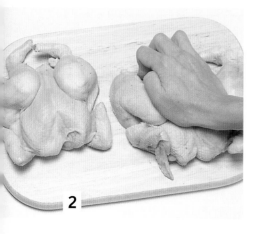

2

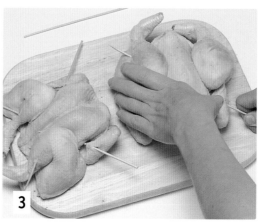

3

6

Thai Noodles & Vegetables with Tofu

INGREDIENTS

Serves 4

225 g/8 oz firm tofu

2 tbsp soy sauce

rind of 1 lime, grated

2 lemon grass stalks

1 red chilli

1 litre/1³/₄ pint vegetable stock

2 slices fresh root ginger, peeled

2 garlic cloves, peeled

2 sprigs of fresh coriander

175 g/6 oz dried thread egg noodles

125 g/4 oz shiitake or button
  mushrooms, sliced if large

2 carrots, peeled and cut
  into matchsticks

125 g/4 oz mangetout

125 g/4 oz bok choy or other
  Chinese leaf

1 tbsp freshly chopped coriander

salt and freshly ground black pepper

coriander sprigs, to garnish

FOOD FACT

Tofu is a curd derived from soya. Recent studies suggest that there are many health benefits to incorporating soya into your diet not least for its cancer-prevention properties.

1 Drain the tofu well and cut into cubes. Put into a shallow dish with the soy sauce and lime rind. Stir well to coat and leave to marinate for 30 minutes.

2 Meanwhile, put the lemon grass and chilli on a chopping board and bruise with the side of a large knife, ensuring the blade is pointing away from you. Put the vegetable stock in a large saucepan and add the lemon grass, chilli, ginger, garlic and coriander. Bring to the boil, cover and simmer gently for 20 minutes.

3 Strain the stock into a clean pan. Return to the boil and add the noodles, tofu and its marinade and the mushrooms. Simmer gently for 4 minutes.

4 Add the carrots, mangetout, bok choy, coriander and simmer for a further 3–4 minutes until the vegetables are just tender. Season to taste with salt and pepper. Garnish with coriander sprigs. Serve immediately.

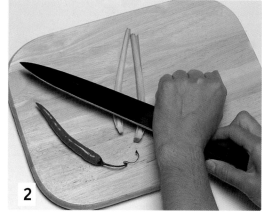

Tagliatelle with Broccoli & Sesame

INGREDIENTS

Serves 2

225 g/8 oz broccoli, cut into florets

125 g/4 oz baby corn

175 g/6 oz dried tagliatelle

1½ tbsp tahini paste

1 tbsp dark soy sauce

1 tbsp dark muscovado sugar

1 tbsp red wine vinegar

1 tbsp sunflower oil

1 garlic clove, peeled and
finely chopped

2.5 cm/1 inch piece fresh root ginger,
peeled and shredded

½ tsp dried chilli flakes

salt and freshly ground black pepper

1 tbsp toasted sesame seeds

slices of radish, to garnish

1 Bring a large saucepan of salted water to the boil and add the broccoli and corn. Return the water to the boil then remove the vegetables at once using a slotted spoon, reserving the water. Plunge them into cold water and drain well. Dry on kitchen paper and reserve.

2 Return the water to the boil. Add the tagliatelle and cook until al dente or according to the packet instructions. Drain well. Run under cold water until cold, then drain well again.

3 Place the tahini, soy sauce, sugar and vinegar into a bowl. Mix well, then reserve. Heat the oil in a wok or large frying pan over a high heat and add the garlic, ginger and chilli flakes and stir-fry for about 30 seconds. Add the broccoli and baby corn and continue to stir-fry for about 3 minutes.

4 Add the tagliatelle to the wok along with the tahini mixture and stir together for a further 1–2 minutes until heated through. Season to taste with salt and pepper. Sprinkle with sesame seeds, garnish with the radish slices and serve immediately.

FOOD FACT

Tahini is made from ground sesame seeds and is generally available in large supermarkets and Middle Eastern shops. It is most often used in hummus.

1

3

4

Pad Thai Noodles with Mushrooms

INGREDIENTS

Serves 4

125 g/4 oz flat rice noodles
  or rice vermicelli
1 tbsp vegetable oil
2 garlic cloves, peeled and
  finely chopped
1 medium egg, lightly beaten
225 g/8 oz mixed mushrooms,
  including shiitake, oyster, field,
  brown and wild mushrooms
2 tbsp lemon juice
1½ tbsp Thai fish sauce
½ tsp sugar
½ tsp cayenne pepper
2 spring onions, trimmed and cut
  into 2.5 cm/1 inch pieces
50 g/2 oz fresh beansprouts

To garnish:
chopped roasted peanuts
freshly chopped coriander

TASTY TIP
An aromatic alternative to this dish is to replace the lemon with lemon grass. Discard the outer leaves, finely chop and add with the other ingredients in step 4.

1 Cook the noodles according to the packet instructions. Drain well and reserve.

2 Heat a wok or large frying pan. Add the oil and garlic. Fry until just golden. Add the egg and stir quickly to break it up.

3 Cook for a few seconds before adding the noodles and mushrooms. Scrape down the sides of the pan to ensure they mix with the egg and garlic.

4 Add the lemon juice, fish sauce, sugar, cayenne pepper, spring onions and half of the beansprouts, stirring quickly all the time.

5 Cook over a high heat for a further 2–3 minutes until everything is heated through.

6 Turn on to a serving plate. Top with the remaining beansprouts. Garnish with the chopped peanuts and coriander and serve immediately.

Pasta with Courgettes, Rosemary & Lemon

INGREDIENTS

Serves 4

350 g/12 oz dried pasta shapes,
  e.g. rigatoni
1½ tbsp good-quality extra-virgin
  olive oil
2 garlic cloves, peeled and
  finely chopped
4 medium courgettes, thinly sliced
1 tbsp freshly chopped rosemary
1 tbsp freshly chopped parsley
zest and juice of 2 lemons
25 g/1 oz pitted black olives,
  roughly chopped
25 g/1 oz pitted green olives,
  roughly chopped
salt and freshly ground black pepper

To garnish:
lemon slices
sprigs of fresh rosemary

1 Bring a large saucepan of salted water to the boil and add the pasta.

2 Return to the boil and cook until al dente or according to the packet instructions.

3 Meanwhile, when the pasta is almost done, heat the oil in a large frying pan and add the garlic.

4 Cook over a medium heat until the garlic just begins to brown. Be careful not to overcook the garlic at this stage or it will become bitter.

5 Add the courgettes, rosemary, parsley and lemon zest and juice. Cook for 3–4 minutes until the courgettes are just tender.

6 Add the olives to the frying pan and stir well. Season to taste with salt and pepper and remove from the heat.

7 Drain the pasta well and add to the frying pan. Stir until thoroughly combined. Garnish with lemon and sprigs of fresh rosemary and serve immediately.

Vegetarian Spaghetti Bolognese

INGREDIENTS

Serves 4

2 tbsp olive oil
1 onion, peeled and finely chopped
1 carrot, peeled and finely chopped
1 celery stick, trimmed and
   finely chopped
225 g/8 oz Quorn mince
150 ml/5 fl oz red wine
300 ml/½ pint vegetable stock
1 tsp mushroom ketchup
4 tbsp tomato purée
350 g/12 oz dried spaghetti
4 tbsp half-fat crème fraîche
salt and freshly ground black pepper
1 tbsp freshly chopped parsley

1 Heat the oil in a large saucepan and add the onion, carrot and celery. Cook gently for 10 minutes, adding a little water if necessary, until softened and starting to brown.

2 Add the Quorn mince and cook for a further 2–3 minutes before adding the red wine. Increase the heat and simmer gently until nearly all the wine has evaporated.

3 Mix together the vegetable stock and mushroom ketchup and add about half to the Quorn mixture along with the tomato purée. Cover and simmer gently for about 45 minutes, adding the remaining stock as necessary.

4 Meanwhile, bring a large pan of salted water to the boil and add the spaghetti. Cook until al dente or according to the packet instructions. Drain well. Remove the sauce from the heat, add the crème fraîche and season to taste with salt and pepper. Stir in the parsley and serve immediately with the pasta.

HELPFUL HINT

Quorn is a mycroprotein that is high in fibre and low in fat. It is derived from the mushroom family and readily takes on any flavour it is put with. An equivalent amount of soya mince can be used in this recipe, whether dried (follow the packet instructions) or frozen.

Spring Vegetable & Herb Risotto

INGREDIENTS

Serves 2–3

1 litre/1³/₄ pint vegetable stock
125 g/4 oz asparagus tips, trimmed
125 g/4 oz baby carrots, scrubbed
50 g/2 oz peas, fresh or frozen
50 g/2 oz fine French beans, trimmed
1 tbsp olive oil
1 onion, peeled and finely chopped
1 garlic clove, peeled and
  finely chopped
2 tsp freshly chopped thyme
225 g/8 oz risotto rice
150 ml/¹/₄ pint white wine
1 tbsp each freshly chopped basil,
  chives and parsley
zest of ¹/₂ lemon
3 tbsp half-fat crème fraîche
salt and freshly ground black pepper

1. Bring the vegetable stock to the boil in a large saucepan and add the asparagus, baby carrots, peas and beans. Bring the stock back to the boil and remove the vegetables at once using a slotted spoon. Rinse under cold running water. Drain again and reserve. Keep the stock hot.

2. Heat the oil in a large deep frying pan and add the onion. Cook over a medium heat for 4–5 minutes until starting to brown. Add the garlic and thyme and cook for a further few seconds. Add the rice and stir well for a minute until the rice is hot and coated in oil.

3. Add the white wine and stir constantly until the wine is almost completely absorbed by the rice. Begin adding the stock a ladleful at a time, stirring well and waiting until the last ladleful has been absorbed before stirring in the next. Add the vegetables after using about half of the stock. Continue until all the stock is used. This will take 20–25 minutes. The rice and vegetables should both be tender.

4. Remove the pan from the heat. Stir in the herbs, lemon zest and crème fraîche. Season to taste with salt and pepper and serve immediately.

FOOD FACT

In Italy, they use different types of rice, such as Arborio and Carnaroli, depending on whether the risotto is vegetable, meat or fish-based.

Baby Onion Risotto

INGREDIENTS

Serves 4

For the baby onions:

1 tbsp olive oil
450 g/1 lb baby onions, peeled and
   halved if large
pinch of sugar
1 tbsp freshly chopped thyme

For the risotto:

1 tbsp olive oil
1 small onion, peeled and
   finely chopped
2 garlic cloves, peeled and
   finely chopped
350 g/12 oz risotto rice
150 ml/¼ pint red wine
1 litre/1¾ pint hot vegetable stock
125 g/4 oz low-fat soft goat's cheese
salt and freshly ground black pepper
sprigs of fresh thyme, to garnish
rocket leaves, to serve

FOOD FACT

To peel baby onions, put into a saucepan of water and bring to the boil. Drain and run under cold water. The skins will loosen and peel easily.

1 For the baby onions, heat the olive oil in a saucepan and add the onions with the sugar. Cover and cook over a low heat, stirring occasionally, for 20–25 minutes until caramelised. Uncover during the last 10 minutes of cooking.

2 Meanwhile, for the risotto, heat the oil in a large frying pan and add the onion. Cook over a medium heat for 5 minutes until softened. Add the garlic and cook for a further 30 seconds.

3 Add the risotto rice and stir well. Add the red wine and stir constantly until the wine is almost completely absorbed by the rice. Begin adding the stock a ladleful at a time, stirring well and waiting until the last ladleful has been absorbed before stirring in the next. It will take 20–25 minutes to add all the stock by which time the rice should be just cooked but still firm. Remove from the heat.

4 Add the thyme to the onions and cook briefly. Increase the heat and allow the onion mixture to bubble for 2–3 minutes until almost evaporated. Add the onion mixture to the risotto along with the goat's cheese. Stir well and season to taste with salt and pepper. Garnish with sprigs of fresh thyme. Serve immediately with the rocket leaves.

Vegetable Biryani

INGREDIENTS

Serves 4

2 tbsp vegetable oil, plus a little extra
   for brushing
2 large onions, peeled and thinly
   sliced lengthways
2 garlic cloves, peeled and
   finely chopped
2.5 cm/1 inch piece fresh root ginger,
   peeled and finely grated
1 small carrot, peeled and cut
   into sticks
1 small parsnip, peeled and diced
1 small sweet potato, peeled
   and diced
1 tbsp medium curry paste
225 g/8 oz basmati rice
4 ripe tomatoes, peeled, deseeded
   and diced
600 ml/1 pint vegetable stock
175 g/6 oz cauliflower florets
50 g/2 oz peas, thawed if frozen
salt and freshly ground black pepper

To garnish:

roasted cashew nuts
raisins
fresh coriander leaves

1 Preheat the oven to 200°C/400°F/Gas Mark 6. Put 1 tablespoon
of the vegetable oil in a large bowl with the onions and toss to coat.
Lightly brush or spray a non-stick baking sheet with a little more oil.
Spread half the onions on the baking sheet and cook at the top of
the preheated oven for 25–30 minutes, stirring regularly, until golden
and crisp. Remove from the oven and reserve for the garnish.

2 Meanwhile, heat a large flameproof casserole dish over a medium
heat and add the remaining oil and onions. Cook for 5–7 minutes
until softened and starting to brown. Add a little water if they start
to stick. Add the garlic and ginger and cook for another minute,
then add the carrot, parsnip and sweet potato. Cook the vegetables
for a further 5 minutes. Add the curry paste and stir for a minute
until everything is coated, then stir in the rice and tomatoes. After
2 minutes add the stock and stir well. Bring to the boil, cover and
simmer over a very gentle heat for about 10 minutes.

3 Add the cauliflower and peas and cook for 8–10 minutes, or
until the rice is tender. Season to taste with salt and pepper.
Serve garnished with the crispy onions, cashew nuts, raisins
and coriander.

Brown Rice Spiced Pilaf

INGREDIENTS

Serves 4

1 tbsp vegetable oil

1 tbsp blanched almonds,
　flaked or chopped

1 onion, peeled and chopped

1 carrot, peeled and diced

225 g/8 oz flat mushrooms,
　sliced thickly

$\frac{1}{4}$ tsp cinnamon

large pinch dried chilli flakes

50 g/2 oz dried apricots,
　roughly chopped

25 g/1 oz currants

zest of 1 orange

350 g/12 oz brown basmati rice

900 ml/1$\frac{1}{2}$ pints vegetable stock

2 tbsp freshly chopped coriander

2 tbsp freshly snipped chives

salt and freshly ground black pepper

snipped chives, to garnish

FOOD FACT

Brown basmati rice, in particular, is one of the best rices to eat, releasing carbohydrate slowly into the blood thereby maintaining the body's energy levels as well as supplying the body with fibre.

1　Preheat the oven to 200°C/400°F/Gas Mark 6. Heat the oil in a large flameproof casserole dish and add the almonds. Cook for 1–2 minutes until just browning. (Be very careful as the nuts will burn very easily).

2　Add the onion and carrot. Cook for 5 minutes until softened and starting to turn brown. Add the mushrooms and cook for a further 5 minutes, stirring often.

3　Add the cinnamon and chilli flakes and cook for about 30 seconds before adding the apricots, currants, orange zest and rice.

4　Stir together well and add the stock. Bring to the boil, cover tightly and transfer to the preheated oven. Cook for 45 minutes until the rice and vegetables are tender.

5　Stir the coriander and chives into the pilaf and season to taste with salt and pepper. Garnish with the extra chives and serve immediately.

2

3

5

Spiced Couscous & Vegetables

INGREDIENTS

Serves 4

1 tbsp olive oil

1 large shallot, peeled and
  finely chopped

1 garlic clove, peeled and
  finely chopped

1 small red pepper, deseeded and cut
  into strips

1 small yellow pepper, deseeded and
  cut into strips

1 small aubergine, diced

1 tsp each turmeric, ground cumin,
  ground cinnamon and paprika

2 tsp ground coriander

large pinch saffron strands

2 tomatoes, peeled, deseeded
  and diced

2 tbsp lemon juice

225 g/8 oz couscous

225 ml/8 fl oz vegetable stock

2 tbsp raisins

2 tbsp whole almonds

2 tbsp freshly chopped parsley

2 tbsp freshly chopped coriander

salt and freshly ground black pepper

1 Heat the oil in a large frying pan and add the shallot and garlic and cook for 2–3 minutes until softened. Add the peppers and aubergine and reduce the heat.

2 Cook for 8–10 minutes until the vegetables are tender, adding a little water if necessary.

3 Test a piece of aubergine to ensure it is cooked through. Add all the spices and cook for a further minute, stirring.

4 Increase the heat and add the tomatoes and lemon juice. Cook for 2–3 minutes until the tomatoes have started to break down. Remove from the heat and leave to cool slightly.

5 Meanwhile, put the couscous into a large bowl. Bring the stock to the boil in a saucepan, then pour over the couscous. Stir well and cover with a clean tea towel.

6 Leave to stand for 7–8 minutes until all the stock is absorbed and the couscous is tender.

7 Uncover the couscous and fluff with a fork. Stir in the vegetable and spice mixture along with the raisins, almonds, parsley and coriander. Season to taste with salt and pepper and serve.

3

5

7

Black Bean Chilli with Avocado Salsa

INGREDIENTS

Serves 4

250 g/9 oz black beans and black-eye
  beans, soaked overnight
2 tbsp olive oil
1 large onion, peeled and chopped
1 red pepper, deseeded and diced
2 garlic cloves, peeled and
  finely chopped
1 red chilli, deseeded and
  finely chopped
2 tsp chilli powder
1 tsp ground cumin
2 tsp ground coriander
400 g can chopped tomatoes
450 ml/³/₄ pint vegetable stock
1 small ripe avocado, diced
¹/₂ small red onion, peeled and
  finely chopped
2 tbsp freshly chopped coriander
juice of 1 lime
1 small tomato, peeled, deseeded
  and diced
salt and freshly ground black pepper
25 g/1 oz dark chocolate

To garnish:

half-fat crème fraîche
lime slices
sprigs of coriander

1 Drain the beans and place in a large saucepan with at least twice their volume of fresh water.

2 Bring slowly to the boil, skimming off any froth that rises to the surface. Boil rapidly for 10 minutes, then reduce the heat and simmer for about 45 minutes, adding more water if necessary. Drain and reserve.

3 Heat the oil in a large saucepan and add the onion and pepper. Cook for 3–4 minutes until softened. Add the garlic and chilli. Cook for 5 minutes, or until the onion and pepper have softened. Add the chilli powder, cumin and coriander and cook for 30 seconds. Add the beans along with the tomatoes and stock.

4 Bring to the boil and simmer uncovered for 40–45 minutes until the beans and vegetables are tender and the sauce has reduced.

5 Mix together the avocado, onion, fresh coriander, lime juice and tomato. Season with salt and pepper and set aside. Remove the chilli from the heat. Break the chocolate into pieces. Sprinkle over the chilli. Leave for 2 minutes. Stir well. Garnish with crème fraîche, lime and coriander. Serve with the avocado salsa.

Boston–style Baked Beans

INGREDIENTS

Serves 8

350 g/12 oz mixed dried pulses, e.g.
  haricot, flageolet, cannellini,
  chickpeas or pinto beans
1 large onion, peeled and
  finely chopped
125 g/4 oz black treacle or molasses
2 tbsp Dijon mustard
2 tbsp light brown soft sugar
125 g/4 oz plain flour
150 g/5 oz fine cornmeal
2 tbsp caster sugar
2½ tsp baking powder
½ tsp salt
2 tbsp freshly chopped thyme
2 medium eggs
200 ml/7 fl oz milk
2 tbsp melted butter
salt and freshly ground black pepper
parsley sprigs, to garnish

1 Preheat the oven to 130°C/250°F/Gas Mark ½. Put the pulses into a large saucepan and cover with at least twice their volume of water. Bring to the boil and simmer for 2 minutes. Leave to stand for 1 hour. Return to the boil and boil rapidly for about 10 minutes. Drain and reserve.

2 Mix together the onion, treacle or molasses, mustard and sugar in a large mixing bowl. Add the drained beans and 300 ml/½ pint fresh water. Stir well, bring to the boil, cover and transfer to the preheated oven for 4 hours in an ovenproof dish, stirring once every hour and adding more water if necessary.

3 When the beans are cooked, remove from the oven and keep warm. Increase the oven temperature to 200°C/400°F/Gas Mark 6. Mix together the plain flour, cornmeal, caster sugar, baking powder, salt and most of the thyme, reserving about one third for garnish. In a separate bowl beat the eggs, then stir in the milk and butter. Pour the wet ingredients on to the dry ones and stir just enough to combine.

4 Pour into a buttered 18 cm/7 inch square cake tin. Sprinkle over the remaining thyme. Bake for 30 minutes until golden and risen or until a toothpick inserted into the centre comes out clean. Cut into squares, then reheat the beans. Season to taste with salt and pepper and serve immediately, garnished with parsley sprigs.

TASTY TIP

For non-vegetarians, add 125 g/ 4 oz of cooked salt pork to the beans as a tasty alternative.

2

3

4

Pumpkin & Chickpea Curry

INGREDIENTS

Serves 4

1 tbsp vegetable oil
1 small onion, peeled and sliced
2 garlic cloves, peeled and
   finely chopped
2.5 cm/1 inch piece root ginger,
   peeled and grated
1 tsp ground coriander
½ tsp ground cumin
½ tsp ground turmeric
¼ tsp ground cinnamon
2 tomatoes, chopped
2 red bird's eye chillies, deseeded
   and finely chopped
450 g/1 lb pumpkin or butternut
   squash flesh, cubed
1 tbsp hot curry paste
300 ml/½ pint vegetable stock
1 large firm banana
400 g can chickpeas, drained
   and rinsed
salt and freshly ground black pepper
1 tbsp freshly chopped coriander
coriander sprigs, to garnish
rice or naan bread, to serve

1 Heat 1 tablespoon of the oil in a saucepan and add the onion. Fry gently for 5 minutes until softened.

2 Add the garlic, ginger and spices and fry for a further minute. Add the chopped tomatoes and chillies and cook for another minute.

3 Add the pumpkin and curry paste and fry gently for 3–4 minutes before adding the stock.

4 Stir well, bring to the boil and simmer for 20 minutes until the pumpkin is tender.

5 Thickly slice the banana and add to the pumpkin along with the chickpeas. Simmer for a further 5 minutes.

6 Season to taste with salt and pepper and add the chopped coriander. Serve immediately, garnished with coriander sprigs and some rice or naan bread.

Roasted Mixed Vegetables with Garlic & Herb Sauce

INGREDIENTS

Serves 4

1 large garlic bulb

1 large onion, peeled and cut
  into wedges

4 small carrots, peeled and quartered

4 small parsnips, peeled

6 small potatoes, scrubbed
  and halved

1 fennel bulb, sliced thickly

4 sprigs of fresh rosemary

4 sprigs of fresh thyme

2 tbsp olive oil

salt and freshly ground black pepper

200 g/7 oz low-fat soft cheese with
  herbs and garlic

4 tbsp milk

zest of ½ lemon

sprigs of thyme, to garnish

TASTY TIP

This dish can be served as a delicious accompaniment to any grilled or roasted fish, seafood or chicken dish. Marinade or drizzle the fish with a little olive oil, lemon juice and rind and mixed herbs.

1 Preheat the oven to 220°C/425°F/Gas Mark 7. Cut the garlic in half horizontally. Put into a large roasting tin with all the vegetables and herbs.

2 Add the oil, season well with salt and pepper and toss together to coat lightly in the oil.

3 Cover with tinfoil and roast in the preheated oven for 50 minutes. Remove the tinfoil and cook for a further 30 minutes until all the vegetables are tender and slightly charred.

4 Remove the tin from the oven and allow to cool.

5 In a small saucepan, melt the low-fat soft cheese together with the milk and lemon zest.

6 Remove the garlic from the roasting tin and squeeze the flesh into a bowl. Mash thoroughly then add to the sauce. Heat through gently. Season the vegetables to taste. Pour some sauce into small ramekins and garnish with 4 sprigs of thyme. Serve immediately with the roasted vegetables and the sauce to dip.

Roasted Butternut Squash

INGREDIENTS

Serves 4

2 small butternut squash
4 garlic cloves, peeled and crushed
1 tbsp olive oil
salt and freshly ground black pepper
1 tbsp walnut oil
4 medium-sized leeks, trimmed,
    cleaned and thinly sliced
1 tbsp black mustard seeds
300 g can cannellini beans, drained
    and rinsed
125 g/4 oz fine French beans, halved
150 ml/¼ pint vegetable stock
50 g/2 oz rocket
2 tbsp freshly snipped chives
fresh chives, to garnish

To serve:
4 tbsp low-fat fromage frais
mixed salad

1 Preheat the oven to 200°C/400°F/Gas Mark 6. Cut the butternut squash in half lengthways and scoop out all of the seeds.

2 Score the squash in a diamond pattern with a sharp knife. Mix the garlic with the olive oil and brush over the cut surfaces of the squash. Season well with salt and pepper. Put on a baking sheet and roast for 40 minutes until tender.

3 Heat the walnut oil in a saucepan and fry the leeks and mustard seeds for 5 minutes.

4 Add the drained cannellini beans, French beans and vegetable stock. Bring to the boil and simmer gently for 5 minutes until the French beans are tender.

5 Remove from the heat and stir in the rocket and chives. Season well. Remove the squash from the oven and allow to cool for 5 minutes. Spoon in the bean mixture. Garnish with a few snipped chives and serve immediately with the fromage frais and a mixed salad.

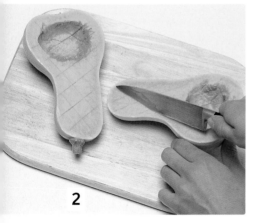

2

3

5

Vegetable Cassoulet

INGREDIENTS

Serves 6

125 g/4 oz dried haricot beans,
   soaked overnight
2 tbsp olive oil
2 garlic cloves, peeled and chopped
225 g/8 oz baby onions, peeled
   and halved
2 carrots, peeled and diced
2 celery sticks, trimmed and
   finely chopped
1 red pepper, deseeded and chopped
175 g/6 oz mixed mushrooms, sliced
1 tbsp each freshly chopped
   rosemary, thyme and sage
150 ml/¼ pint red wine
4 tbsp tomato purée
1 tbsp dark soy sauce
salt and freshly ground black pepper
50 g/2 oz fresh breadcrumbs
1 tbsp freshly chopped parsley
basil sprigs, to garnish

1 Preheat the oven to 190°C/375°F/Gas Mark 5. Drain the haricot beans and place in a saucepan with 1.1 litres/2 pints of fresh water. Bring to the boil and boil rapidly for 10 minutes. Reduce the heat and simmer gently for 45 minutes. Drain the beans, reserving 300 ml/½ pint of the liquid.

2 Heat 1 tablespoon of the oil in a flameproof casserole dish and add the garlic, onions, carrot, celery and red pepper. Cook gently for 10–12 minutes until tender and starting to brown. Add a little water if the vegetables start to stick. Add the mushrooms and cook for a further 5 minutes until softened. Add the herbs and stir briefly.

3 Stir in the red wine and boil rapidly for about 5 minutes until reduced and syrupy. Stir in the reserved beans and their liquid, tomato purée and soy sauce. Season to taste with salt and pepper.

4 Mix together the breadcrumbs and parsley with the remaining 1 tablespoon of oil. Scatter this mixture evenly over the top of the stew. Cover loosely with foil and transfer to the preheated oven. Cook for 30 minutes. Carefully remove the foil and cook for a further 15–20 minutes until the topping is crisp and golden. Serve immediately, garnished with basil sprigs.

HELPFUL HINT

If cooking dried haricot beans is too time-consuming, substitute with canned beans instead.

Creamy Puy Lentils

INGREDIENTS

Serves 4

225 g/8 oz Puy lentils
1 tbsp olive oil
1 garlic clove, peeled and
  finely chopped
zest and juice of 1 lemon
1 tsp whole-grain mustard
1 tbsp freshly chopped tarragon
3 tbsp half-fat crème fraîche
salt and freshly ground black pepper
2 small tomatoes, deseeded
  and chopped
50 g/2 oz pitted black olives
1 tbsp freshly chopped parsley

To garnish:

sprigs of fresh tarragon
lemon wedges

FOOD FACT

Puy lentils are smaller and fatter than green lentils and have a pretty mottled colouring, ranging from gold through to green. They keep their shape and firm texture when cooked. They may not always be French, however, as this type of lentil is also grown extensively in Canada.

1 Put the lentils in a saucepan with plenty of cold water and bring to the boil.

2 Boil rapidly for 10 minutes, reduce the heat and simmer gently for a further 20 minutes until just tender. Drain well.

3 Meanwhile, prepare the dressing. Heat the oil in a frying pan over a medium heat.

4 Add the garlic and cook for about a minute until just beginning to brown. Add the lemon zest and juice.

5 Add the mustard and cook for a further 30 seconds.

6 Add the tarragon and crème fraîche and season to taste with salt and pepper.

7 Simmer and add the drained lentils, tomatoes and olives.

8 Transfer to a serving dish and sprinkle the chopped parsley on top.

9 Garnish the lentils with the tarragon sprigs and the lemon wedges and serve immediately.

Peperonata

INGREDIENTS

Serves 6

2 red peppers
2 yellow peppers
450 g/1 lb waxy potatoes
1 large onion
2 tbsp good-quality virgin olive oil
700 g/1½ lb tomatoes, peeled,
   deseeded and chopped
2 small courgettes
50 g/2 oz pitted black
   olives, quartered
small handful basil leaves
salt and freshly ground black pepper
crusty bread, to serve

FOOD FACT

This dish is delicious served with Parmesan melba toasts. To make simply remove the crusts from 4 slices of thin white bread. Lightly toast and allow to cool before splitting each piece in half by slicing horizontally. Cut diagonally into triangles, place under a hot grill and toast each side for a few minutes until golden and curling at the edges. Sprinkle with finely grated fresh Parmesan cheese and melt under the grill.

1 Prepare the peppers by halving them lengthways and removing the stems, seeds, and membranes.

2 Cut the peppers lengthways into strips about 1 cm/½ inch wide. Peel the potatoes and cut into rough dice, about 2.5–3 cm/1–1¼ inch across. Cut the onion lengthways into 8 wedges.

3 Heat the olive oil in a large saucepan over a medium heat.

4 Add the onion and cook for about 5 minutes, or until starting to brown.

5 Add the peppers, potatoes, tomatoes, courgettes, black olives and about 4 torn basil leaves. Season to taste with salt and pepper.

6 Stir the mixture, cover and cook over a very low heat for about 40 minutes, or until the vegetables are tender but still hold their shape. Garnish with the remaining basil. Transfer to a serving bowl and serve immediately, with chunks of crusty bread.

1

4

5

Mushroom Stew

INGREDIENTS

Serves 4

15 g/¹/₂ oz dried
  porcini mushrooms
900 g/2 lb assorted fresh
  mushrooms, wiped
2 tbsp good-quality virgin olive oil
1 onion, peeled and finely chopped
2 garlic cloves, peeled and
  finely chopped
1 tbsp fresh thyme leaves
pinch of ground cloves
salt and freshly ground black pepper
700 g/1¹/₂ lb tomatoes, peeled,
  deseeded and chopped
225 g/8 oz instant polenta
600 ml/1 pint vegetable stock
3 tbsp freshly chopped mixed herbs
sprigs of parsley, to garnish

TASTY TIP

For a dinner party version of this recipe, add a generous splash of vegetarian red wine with the soaking liquid in step 5 and just before serving, remove from the heat and stir in 2 tablespoons of low-fat Greek yogurt.

1 Soak the porcini mushrooms in a small bowl of hot water for 20 minutes.

2 Drain reserving the porcini mushrooms and their soaking liquor. Cut the fresh mushrooms in half and reserve.

3 In a saucepan, heat the oil and add the onion.

4 Cook gently for 5–7 minutes until softened. Add the garlic, thyme and cloves and continue cooking for 2 minutes.

5 Add all the mushrooms and cook for 8–10 minutes until the mushrooms have softened, stirring often. Season to taste with salt and pepper and add the tomatoes and the reserved soaking liquid.

6 Simmer, partly-covered, over a low heat for about 20 minutes until thickened. Adjust the seasoning to taste.

7 Meanwhile, cook the polenta according to the packet instructions using the vegetable stock. Stir in the herbs and divide between 4 dishes.

8 Ladle the mushrooms over the polenta, garnish with the parsley and serve immediately.

Huevos Rancheros

INGREDIENTS

Serves 4

2 tbsp olive oil

1 large onion, peeled and
  finely chopped

1 red pepper, deseeded and
  finely chopped

2 garlic cloves, peeled and
  finely chopped

2–4 green chillies, deseeded and
  finely chopped

1 tsp ground cumin

1 tsp chilli powder

2 tsp ground coriander

2 tbsp freshly
  chopped coriander

700 g/1½ lb ripe plum tomatoes,
  peeled, deseeded and roughly
  chopped

¼ tsp sugar

8 small eggs

4–8 flour tortillas

salt and freshly ground
  black pepper

sprigs of fresh coriander,
  to garnish

refried beans, to
  serve (optional)

1 Heat the oil in a large heavy-based saucepan. Add the onion and pepper and cook over a medium heat for 10 minutes.

2 Add the garlic, chillies, ground cumin, chilli powder and chopped coriander and cook for a further minute.

3 Add the tomatoes and sugar. Stir well, cover and cook gently for 20 minutes. Uncover and cook for a further 20 minutes.

4 Lightly poach the eggs in a large frying pan, filled with gently simmering water. Drain well and keep warm.

5 Place the tortillas briefly under a preheated hot grill. Turning once, then remove from the grill when crisp.

6 Add the freshly chopped coriander to the tomato sauce and season to taste with salt and pepper.

7 To serve, arrange two tortillas on each serving plate, top with two eggs and spoon the sauce over. Garnish with sprigs of fresh coriander and serve immediately with warmed refried beans, if liked.

2

4

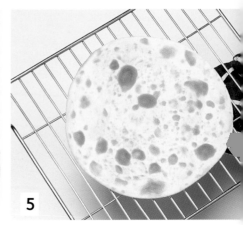

5

Aubergine & Yogurt Dip

INGREDIENTS

Makes 600 ml/1 pint

2 x 225 g/8 oz aubergines

1 tbsp light olive oil

1 tbsp lemon juice

2 garlic cloves, peeled
  and crushed

190 g jar pimientos, drained

150 ml/¼ pint low-fat
  natural yogurt

salt and freshly ground
  black pepper

25 g/1 oz black olives, pitted and
  chopped

225 g/8 oz cauliflower florets

225 g/8 oz broccoli florets

125 g/4 oz carrots, peeled and cut
  into 5 cm/2 inch strips

TASTY TIP

Why not also serve pieces of warmed, unleavened bread such as naan or pitta with this dip. To warm the bread, preheat the oven to 200°C/400°F/Gas Mark 6, wrap in preheated tinfoil and place in the oven for 5–7 minutes depending on the size of the bread.

1   Preheat the oven to 200°C/400°F/Gas Mark 6. Pierce the skin of the aubergines with a fork and place on a baking tray. Cook for 40 minutes or until very soft.

2   Cool the aubergines, then cut in half, scoop out the flesh and tip into a bowl.

3   Mash the aubergine with the olive oil, lemon juice and garlic until smooth or blend for a few seconds in a food processor.

4   Chop the pimientos into small dice and add to the mixture.

5   When blended add the yogurt. Stir well and season to taste with salt and pepper.

6   Add the chopped olives and leave in the refrigerator to chill for at least 30 minutes.

7   Place the cauliflower and broccoli florets and carrot strips into a pan and cover with boiling water. Simmer for 2 minutes, then rinse in cold water. Drain and serve as crudités to accompany the dip.

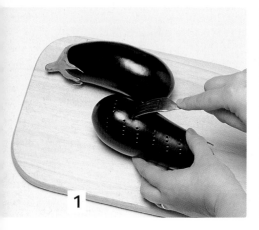

1

3

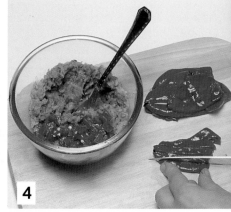

4

Bulghur Wheat Salad with Minty Lemon Dressing

INGREDIENTS

Serves 4

125 g/4 oz bulghur wheat
10 cm /4 inch piece cucumber
2 shallots, peeled
125 g/4 oz baby sweetcorn
3 ripe but firm tomatoes

Dressing:

grated rind of 1 lemon
3 tbsp lemon juice
3 tbsp freshly chopped mint
2 tbsp freshly chopped parsley
1–2 tsp clear honey
2 tbsp sunflower oil
salt and freshly ground black pepper

1 Place the bulghur wheat in a saucepan and cover with boiling water.

2 Simmer for about 10 minutes, then drain thoroughly and turn into a serving bowl.

3 Cut the cucumber into small dice, chop the shallots finely and reserve. Steam the sweetcorn over a pan of boiling water for 10 minutes or until tender. Drain and slice into thick chunks.

4 Cut a cross on the top of each tomato and place in boiling water until their skins start to peel away.

5 Remove the skins and the seeds and cut the tomatoes into small dice.

6 Make the dressing by briskly whisking all the ingredients in a small bowl until mixed well.

7 When the bulghur wheat has cooled a little, add all the prepared vegetables and stir in the dressing. Season to taste with salt and pepper and serve.

FOOD FACT

This dish is loosely based on the Middle Eastern dish tabbouleh, a type of salad in which all the ingredients are mixed together and served cold.

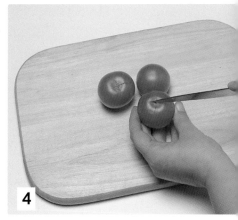

Carrot & Parsnip Terrine

INGREDIENTS

Serves 8-10

550 g/1¼ lb carrots, peeled
  and chopped
450 g/1 lb parsnips, peeled
  and chopped
6 tbsp half-fat crème fraîche
450 g/1 lb spinach, rinsed
1 tbsp brown sugar
1 tbsp freshly chopped parsley
½ tsp freshly grated nutmeg
salt and freshly ground black pepper
6 medium eggs
sprigs of fresh basil, to garnish

Tomato coulis:

450 g/1 lb ripe tomatoes, deseeded
  and chopped
1 medium onion, peeled and
  finely chopped

1. Preheat the oven to 200°C/400°F/Gas Mark 6. Oil and line a 900 g/2 lb loaf tin with non-stick baking paper. Cook the carrots and parsnips in boiling salted water for 10–15 minutes or until very tender. Drain and purée separately. Add 2 tablespoons of crème fraîche to both the carrots and the parsnips.

2. Steam the spinach for 5–10 minutes or until very tender. Drain and squeeze out as much liquid as possible, then stir in the remaining crème fraîche.

3. Add the brown sugar to the carrot purée, the parsley to the parsnip mixture and the nutmeg to the spinach. Season all to taste with salt and pepper.

4. Beat 2 eggs, add to the spinach and turn into the prepared tin. Add another 2 beaten eggs to the carrot mixture and layer carefully on top of the spinach. Beat the remaining eggs into the parsnip purée and layer on top of the terrine.

5. Place the tin in a baking dish and pour in enough hot water to come halfway up the sides of the tin. Bake in the preheated oven for 1 hour until a skewer inserted into the centre comes out clean.

6. Leave the terrine to cool for at least 30 minutes. Run a sharp knife around the edges. Turn out on to a dish and reserve.

7. Make the tomato coulis by simmering the tomatoes and onions together for 5–10 minutes until slightly thickened.

8. Season to taste. Blend well in a liquidiser or food processor and serve as an accompaniment to the terrine. Garnish with sprigs of basil and serve.

3

4

7

Chinese Salad with Soy & Ginger Dressing

INGREDIENTS

Serves 4

1 head of Chinese cabbage
200 g can water chestnuts, drained
6 spring onions, trimmed
4 ripe but firm cherry tomatoes
125 g/4 oz mangetout
125 g/4 oz beansprouts
2 tbsp freshly chopped coriander

Soy and ginger dressing:

2 tbsp sunflower oil
4 tbsp light soy sauce
2.5 cm/1 inch piece root ginger,
  peeled and finely grated
zest and juice of 1 lemon
salt and freshly ground black pepper
crusty white bread, to serve

1 Rinse and finely shred the Chinese cabbage and place in a serving dish.

2 Slice the water chestnuts into small slivers and cut the spring onions diagonally into 2.5 cm/1 inch lengths, then split lengthways into thin strips.

3 Cut the tomatoes in half and then slice each half into 3 wedges and reserve.

4 Simmer the mangetout in boiling water for 2 minutes until beginning to soften, drain and cut in half diagonally.

5 Arrange the water chestnuts, spring onions, mangetout, tomatoes and beansprouts on top of the shredded Chinese cabbage. Garnish with the freshly chopped coriander.

6 Make the dressing by whisking all the ingredients together in a small bowl until mixed thoroughly. Serve with the bread and the salad.

2

3

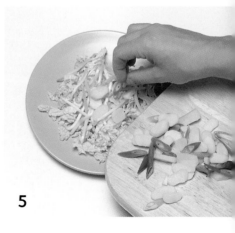

5

Curly Endive & Seafood Salad

INGREDIENTS

Serves 4

1 head of curly endive lettuce
2 green peppers
12.5 cm/5 inch piece cucumber
125 g/4 oz squid, cleaned and cut into
   thin rings
225 g/8 oz baby asparagus spears
125 g/4 oz smoked salmon slices, cut
   into wide strips
175 g/6 oz fresh cooked mussels in
   their shells

Lemon dressing:

2 tbsp sunflower oil
1 tbsp white wine vinegar
5 tbsp fresh lemon juice
1–2 tsp caster sugar
1 tsp mild whole-grain mustard
salt and freshly ground black pepper

To garnish:

slices of lemon
sprigs of fresh coriander

1 Rinse and tear the endive into small pieces and arrange on a serving platter.

2 Remove the seeds from the peppers and cut the peppers and the cucumber into small dice. Sprinkle over the endive.

3 Bring a saucepan of water to the boil and add the squid rings. Bring the pan up to the boil again, then switch off the heat and leave it to stand for 5 minutes. Then drain and rinse thoroughly in cold water.

4 Cook the asparagus in boiling water for 5 minutes or until tender but just crisp. Arrange with the squid, smoked salmon and mussels on top of the salad.

5 To make the lemon dressing, put all the ingredients into a screw-topped jar or into a small bowl and mix thoroughly until the ingredients are combined.

6 Spoon 3 tablespoons of the dressing over the salad and serve the remainder in a small jug. Garnish the salad with slices of lemon and sprigs of coriander and serve.

2

3

4

Warm Fruity Rice Salad

INGREDIENTS

Serves 4

175 g/6 oz mixed basmati and
   wild rice
125 g/4 oz skinless chicken breast
300 ml/¹/₂ pint chicken or
   vegetable stock
125 g/4 oz ready-to-eat dried apricots
125 g/4 oz ready-to-eat dried dates
3 sticks celery

Dressing:

2 tbsp sunflower oil
1 tbsp white wine vinegar
4 tbsp lemon juice
1–2 tsp clear honey, warmed
1 tsp Dijon mustard
freshly ground black pepper

To garnish:

6 spring onions
sprigs of fresh coriander

HELPFUL HINT

It is very important that the chicken is cooked properly. The best way to test is to cut into the thickest part of the meat and check that there is no pinkness.

1 Place the rice in a pan of boiling salted water and cook for 15–20 minutes or until tender. Rinse thoroughly with boiling water and reserve.

2 Meanwhile wipe the chicken and place in a shallow saucepan with the stock.

3 Bring to the boil, cover and simmer for about 15 minutes or until the chicken is cooked thoroughly and the juices run clear.

4 Leave the chicken in the stock until cool enough to handle, then cut into thin slices.

5 Chop the apricots and dates into small pieces. Peel any tough membranes from the outside of the celery and chop into dice. Fold the apricots, dates, celery and sliced chicken into the warm rice.

6 Make the dressing by whisking all the ingredients together in a small bowl until mixed thoroughly. Pour 2–3 tablespoons over the rice and stir in gently and evenly. Serve the remaining dressing separately.

7 Trim and chop the spring onions. Sprinkle the spring onions over the top of the salad and garnish with the sprigs of coriander. Serve while still warm.

2

5

6

Fusilli Pasta with Spicy Tomato Salsa

INGREDIENTS

Serves 4

6 large ripe tomatoes

2 tbsp lemon juice

2 tbsp lime juice

grated rind of 1 lime

2 shallots, peeled and finely chopped

2 garlic cloves, peeled and
  finely chopped

1–2 red chillies

1–2 green chillies

450 g/1 lb fresh fusilli pasta

4 tbsp half-fat crème fraîche

2 tbsp freshly chopped basil

sprig of oregano, to garnish

FOOD FACT

Pasta is an excellent source of complex carbohydrate and is vital for a healthy lifestyle. Complex carbohydrates are broken down by the body more slowly than simple carbohydrates (contained in cakes, sweets and biscuits) and provide a sustained source of energy.

1 Place the tomatoes in a bowl and cover with boiling water. Allow to stand until the skins start to peel away.

2 Remove the skins from the tomatoes, divide each tomato in four and remove all the seeds. Chop the flesh into small dice and put in a small pan. Add the lemon and lime juice and the grated lime rind and stir well.

3 Add the chopped shallots and garlic. Remove the seeds carefully from the chillies, chop finely and add to the pan.

4 Bring to the boil and simmer gently for 5–10 minutes until the salsa has thickened slightly.

5 Reserve the salsa to allow the flavours to develop while the pasta is cooking.

6 Bring a large pan of water to the boil and add the pasta. Simmer gently for 3–4 minutes or until the pasta is just tender.

7 Drain the pasta and rinse in boiling water. Top with a large spoonful of salsa and a small spoonful of crème fraîche. Garnish with the chopped basil and oregano and serve immediately.

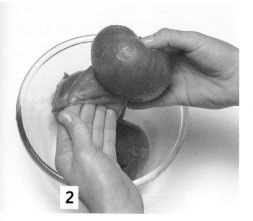
2

3

6

Hot & Spicy Red Cabbage with Apples

INGREDIENTS

Serves 8

900 g/2 lb red cabbage, cored
  and shredded

450 g/1 lb onions, peeled and
  finely sliced

450 g/1 lb cooking apples, peeled,
  cored and finely sliced

½ tsp mixed spice

1 tsp ground cinnamon

2 tbsp light soft brown sugar

salt and freshly ground black pepper

grated rind of 1 large orange

1 tbsp fresh orange juice

50 ml/2 fl oz medium sweet cider
  (or apple juice)

2 tbsp wine vinegar

To serve:

half-fat crème fraîche

freshly ground black pepper

1 Preheat the oven to 150°C/300°F/Gas Mark 2. Put just enough cabbage in a large casserole dish to cover the base evenly.

2 Place a layer of the onions and apples on top of the cabbage.

3 Sprinkle a little of the mixed spice, cinnamon and sugar over the top. Season with salt and pepper.

4 Spoon over a small portion of the orange rind, orange juice and the cider.

5 Continue to layer the casserole dish with the ingredients in the same order until used up.

6 Pour the vinegar as evenly as possible over the top layer of the ingredients.

7 Cover the casserole dish with a close-fitting lid and bake in the preheated oven, stirring occasionally, for 2 hours until the cabbage is moist and tender. Serve immediately with the crème fraîche and black pepper.

2

3

7

Marinated Vegetable Kebabs

INGREDIENTS

Serves 4

2 small courgettes, cut into
  2 cm/³/₄ inch pieces
¹/₂ green pepper, deseeded and cut
  into 2.5 cm/1 inch pieces
¹/₂ red pepper, deseeded and cut into
  2.5 cm /1 inch pieces
¹/₂ yellow pepper, deseeded and cut
  into 2.5 cm/1 inch pieces
8 baby onions, peeled
8 button mushrooms
8 cherry tomatoes
freshly chopped parsley, to garnish
freshly cooked couscous, to serve

Marinade:

1 tbsp light olive oil
4 tbsp dry sherry
2 tbsp light soy sauce
1 red chilli, deseeded and
  finely chopped
2 garlic cloves, peeled and crushed
2.5 cm/1 inch piece root ginger,
  peeled and finely grated

1 Place the courgettes, peppers and baby onions in a pan of just boiled water. Bring back to the boil and simmer for about 30 seconds.

2 Drain and rinse the cooked vegetables in cold water and dry on absorbent kitchen paper.

3 Thread the cooked vegetables and the mushrooms and tomatoes alternately on to skewers and place in a large shallow dish.

4 Make the marinade by whisking all the ingredients together until thoroughly blended. Pour the marinade evenly over the kebabs, then chill in the refrigerator for at least 1 hour. Spoon the marinade over the kebabs occasionally during this time.

5 Place the kebabs in a hot griddle pan or on a hot barbecue and cook gently for 10–12 minutes. Turn the kebabs frequently and brush with the marinade when needed. When the vegetables are tender, sprinkle over the chopped parsley and serve immediately with couscous.

Pumpkin Pâté

INGREDIENTS

Serves 8-10

450 g/1 lb fresh pumpkin flesh
(when in season), peeled, or
425 g can pumpkin purée
1 tsp sunflower oil
1 small onion, peeled and
finely chopped
½ orange pepper, deseeded and
finely chopped
2 medium eggs, beaten
3 tbsp low-fat natural yogurt
125 g/4 oz low-fat hard cheese
(such as Edam or reduced-fat
Gouda cheese), grated
50 g/2 oz wheatgerm
1 tbsp freshly chopped oregano
salt and freshly ground black pepper
fresh salad leaves and crusty bread,
to serve

TASTY TIP

This pâté, after being mixed together in step 4, could also be used to stuff fresh pasta. Serve the pasta tossed in a little extra-virgin olive oil and some roughly torn fresh sage leaves.

1 Preheat the oven to 180°C/350°F/Gas Mark 4. Oil and line a 900 ml/1½ pint oblong dish or loaf tin. Cut the pumpkin flesh into cubes and place in a pan of boiling water.

2 Simmer for 20 minutes or until the pumpkin is very tender. Drain and leave to cool, then mash well to form a purée.

3 Heat the oil in a non-stick frying pan and cook the chopped onion and pepper for about 4 minutes, until softened.

4 Mix together the puréed pumpkin, softened vegetables, eggs and yogurt. Add the cheese, wheatgerm and chopped oregano. Season well with salt and pepper.

5 When the pumpkin mixture is well blended, spoon it into the prepared tin and stand in a baking dish. Fill the tray with hot water to come halfway up the sides of the tin and carefully place in the preheated oven.

6 Bake for about 1 hour or until firm, then leave to cool. Chill for 30 minutes before turning out on to a serving plate. Serve with crusty bread and a fresh salad.

2

3

4

Spanish Baked Tomatoes

INGREDIENTS

Serves 4

175 g/6 oz whole-grain rice
600 ml/1 pint vegetable stock
2 tsp sunflower oil
2 shallots, peeled and finely chopped
1 garlic clove, peeled and crushed
1 green pepper, deseeded and cut
   into small dice
1 red chilli, deseeded and
   finely chopped
50 g/2 oz button mushrooms,
   finely chopped
1 tbsp freshly chopped oregano
salt and freshly ground black pepper
4 large ripe beef tomatoes
1 large egg, beaten
1 tsp caster sugar
basil leaves, to garnish
crusty bread, to serve

TASTY TIP

This dish is also delicious when made with meat. Add 125 g/4 oz of minced beef in step 2. Heat the frying pan and dry-fry the meat on a high heat until cooked through and brown, before adding the rest of the ingredients.

1. Preheat the oven to 180°C/350°F/ Gas Mark 4. Place the rice in a saucepan, pour over the vegetable stock and bring to the boil. Simmer for 30 minutes or until the rice is tender. Drain and turn into a mixing bowl.

2. Add 1 teaspoon of sunflower oil to a small non-stick pan and gently fry the shallots, garlic, pepper, chilli and mushrooms for 2 minutes. Add to the rice with the chopped oregano. Season with plenty of salt and pepper.

3. Slice the top off each tomato. Cut and scoop out the flesh, removing the hard core. Pass the tomato flesh through a sieve. Add 1 tablespoon of the juice to the rice mixture. Stir in the beaten egg and mix. Sprinkle a little sugar in the base of each tomato. Pile the rice mixture into the shells.

4. Place the tomatoes in a baking dish and pour a little cold water around them. Replace their lids and drizzle a few drops of sunflower oil over the tops.

5. Bake in the preheated oven for about 25 minutes. Garnish with the basil leaves and season with black pepper and serve immediately with crusty bread.

2

3

3

Stuffed Onions with Pine Nuts

INGREDIENTS

Serves 4

4 medium onions, peeled
2 garlic cloves, peeled and crushed
2 tbsp fresh brown breadcrumbs
2 tbsp white breadcrumbs
25 g/1 oz sultanas
25 g/1 oz pine nuts
50 g/2 oz low-fat hard cheese such as
   Edam, grated
2 tbsp freshly chopped parsley
1 medium egg, beaten
salt and freshly ground black pepper
salad leaves, to serve

1 Preheat the oven to 200°C/400°F/Gas Mark 6. Bring a pan of water to the boil, add the onions and cook gently for about 15 minutes.

2 Drain well. Allow the onions to cool, then slice each one in half horizontally.

3 Scoop out most of the onion flesh but leave a reasonably firm shell.

4 Chop up 4 tablespoons of the onion flesh and place in a bowl with the crushed garlic, breadcrumbs, sultanas, pine nuts, grated cheese and parsley.

5 Mix the breadcrumb mixture together thoroughly. Bind together with as much of the beaten egg as necessary to make a firm filling. Season to taste with salt and pepper.

6 Pile the mixture back into the onion shells and top with the grated cheese. Place on an oiled baking tray and cook in the preheated oven for 20–30 minutes or until golden brown. Serve immediately with the salad leaves.

FOOD FACT
While this dish is delicious on its own, it also compliments barbecued meat and fish. The onion takes on a mellow, nutty flavour when baked.

3

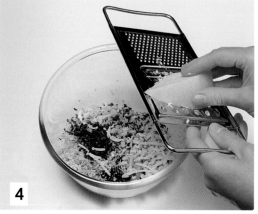

4

6

Warm Leek & Tomato Salad

INGREDIENTS

Serves 4

450 g/1 lb trimmed baby leeks
225 g/8 oz ripe, but firm tomatoes
2 shallots, peeled and cut into
  thin wedges

Honey and lime dressing:

2 tbsp clear honey
grated rind of 1 lime
4 tbsp lime juice
1 tbsp light olive oil
1 tsp Dijon mustard
salt and freshly ground black pepper

To garnish:

freshly chopped tarragon
freshly chopped basil

HELPFUL HINT

Really flavoursome tomatoes can make all the difference to tomato dishes. It is worth using plum or vittoria tomatoes as they have been left on the vine longer to ripen and therefore have a better flavour.

1   Trim the leeks so that they are all the same length. Place in a steamer over a pan of boiling water and steam for 8 minutes or until just tender.

2   Drain the leeks thoroughly and arrange in a shallow serving dish.

3   Make a cross in the top of the tomatoes, place in a bowl and cover them with boiling water until their skins start to peel away. Remove from the bowl and carefully remove the skins.

4   Cut the tomatoes into 4 and remove the seeds, then chop into small dice. Spoon over the top of the leeks together with the shallots.

5   In a small bowl make the dressing by whisking the honey, lime rind, lime juice, olive oil, mustard and salt and pepper. Pour 3 tablespoons of the dressing over the leeks and tomatoes and garnish with the tarragon and basil. Serve while the leeks are still warm, with the remaining dressing served separately.

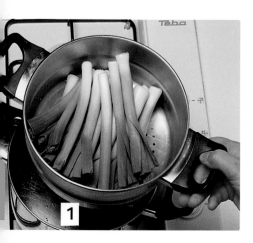

1

3

5

Winter Coleslaw

INGREDIENTS

Serves 6

175 g/6 oz white cabbage
1 medium red onion, peeled
175 g/6 oz carrot, peeled
175 g/6 oz celeriac, peeled
2 celery stalks, trimmed
75 g/3 oz golden sultanas

Yogurt & herb dressing:

150 ml/¼ pint low-fat
  natural yogurt
1 garlic clove, peeled
  and crushed
1 tbsp lemon juice
1 tsp clear honey
1 tbsp freshly snipped chives

TASTY TIP

To make cheese coleslaw, simply replace the sultanas with 75 g/ 3 oz of reduced-fat cheese. Whether the winter or cheese variety, coleslaw is particularly good with baked potatoes and a little low-fat spread.

1 Remove the hard core from the cabbage with a small knife and shred finely.

2 Slice the onion finely and coarsely grate the carrot.

3 Place the raw vegetables in a large bowl and mix together.

4 Cut the celeriac into thin strips and simmer in boiling water for about 2 minutes.

5 Drain the celeriac and rinse thoroughly with cold water.

6 Chop the celery and add to the bowl with the celeriac and sultanas and mix well.

7 Make the yogurt and herb dressing by briskly whisking the yogurt, garlic, lemon juice, honey and chives together.

8 Pour the dressing over the top of the salad. Stir the vegetables thoroughly to coat evenly and serve.

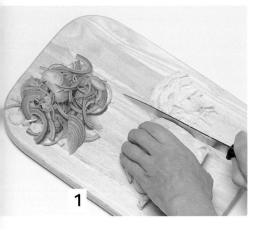

1

4

6

Mediterranean Feast

INGREDIENTS

Serves 4

1 small iceberg lettuce
225 g/8 oz French beans
225 g/8 oz baby new
   potatoes, scrubbed
4 medium eggs
1 green pepper
1 medium onion, peeled
200 g can tuna in brine, drained and
   flaked into small pieces
50 g/2 oz low-fat hard cheese, such
   as Edam, cut into small cubes
8 ripe but firm cherry
   tomatoes, quartered
50 g/2 oz black pitted olives, halved
freshly chopped basil, to garnish

Lime vinaigrette:

3 tbsp light olive oil
2 tbsp white wine vinegar
4 tbsp lime juice
grated rind of 1 lime
1 tsp Dijon mustard
1-2 tsp caster sugar
salt and freshly ground
   black pepper

1 Cut the lettuce into 4 and remove the hard core. Tear into bite-sized pieces and arrange on a large serving platter or 4 individual plates.

2 Cook the French beans in boiling salted water for 8 minutes and the potatoes for 10 minutes or until tender. Drain and rinse in cold water until cool, then cut both the beans and potatoes in half with a sharp knife.

3 Boil the eggs for 10 minutes, then rinse thoroughly under a cold running tap until cool. Remove the shells under water and cut each egg into 4.

4 Remove the seeds from the pepper and cut into thin strips and finely chop the onion.

5 Arrange the beans, potatoes, eggs, peppers and onion on top of the lettuce. Add the tuna, cheese and tomatoes. Sprinkle over the olives and garnish with the basil.

6 To make the vinaigrette, place all the ingredients in a screw-topped jar and shake vigorously until everything is mixed thoroughly. Spoon 4 tablespoons over the top of the prepared salad and serve the remainder separately.

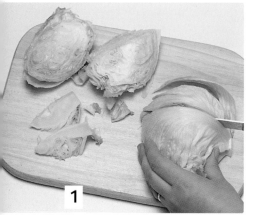
1

4

5

Beetroot & Potato Medley

INGREDIENTS

Serves 4

350 g/12 oz raw baby beetroot
½ tsp sunflower oil
225 g/8 oz new potatoes
½ cucumber, peeled
3 tbsp white wine vinegar
150 ml/5 fl oz natural low-fat yogurt
salt and freshly ground black pepper
fresh salad leaves
1 tbsp freshly snipped chives,
   to garnish

1 Preheat the oven to 180°C/350°F/Gas Mark 4. Scrub the beetroot thoroughly and place on a baking tray.

2 Brush the beetroot with a little oil and cook for 1½ hours or until a skewer is easily insertable into the beetroot. Allow to cool a little, then remove the skins.

3 Cook the potatoes in boiling water for about 10 minutes. Rinse in cold water and drain. Reserve the potatoes until cool. Dice evenly.

4 Cut the cucumber into cubes and place in a mixing bowl. Chop the beetroot into small cubes and add to the bowl with the reserved potatoes. Gently mix the vegetables together.

5 Mix together the vinegar and yogurt and season to taste with a little salt and pepper. Pour over the vegetables and combine gently.

6 Arrange on a bed of salad leaves garnished with the snipped chives and serve.

HELPFUL HINT

Beetroot can also be cooked in the microwave. Place in a microwaveable bowl. Add sufficient water to come halfway up the sides of the bowl. Cover and cook for 10–15 minutes on high. Leave for 5 minutes before removing the paper. Cook before peeling.

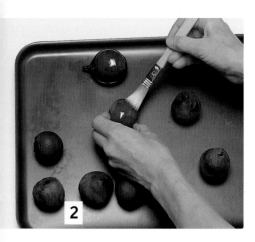

2

3

4

Light Ratatouille

INGREDIENTS

Serves 4

1 red pepper
2 courgettes, trimmed
1 small aubergine, trimmed
1 onion, peeled
2 ripe tomatoes
50 g/2 oz button mushrooms, wiped
  and halved or quartered
200 ml/7 fl oz tomato juice
1 tbsp freshly chopped basil
salt and freshly ground black pepper

1   Deseed the peppers, remove the membrane with a small sharp knife and cut into small dice. Thickly slice the courgettes and cut the aubergine into small dice. Slice the onion into rings.

2   Place the tomatoes in boiling water until their skins begin to peel away.

3   Remove the skins from the tomatoes, cut into quarters and remove the seeds.

4   Place all the vegetables in a saucepan with the tomato juice and basil. Season to taste with salt and pepper.

5   Bring to the boil, cover and simmer for 15 minutes or until the vegetables are tender.

6   Remove the vegetables with a slotted spoon and arrange in a serving dish.

7   Bring the liquid in the pan to the boil and boil for 20 seconds until it is slightly thickened. Season the sauce to taste with salt and pepper.

8   Pass the sauce through a sieve to remove some of the seeds and pour over the vegetables. Serve the ratatouille hot or cold.

TASTY TIP

This dish would be perfect, served as an accompaniment to any of the baked fish dishes in this book. It is also delicious in an omelette or as a jacket potato filling.

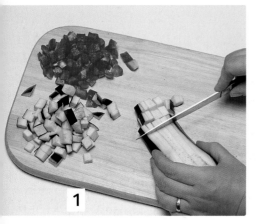

1

4

6

Sicilian Baked Aubergine

INGREDIENTS

Serves 4

1 large aubergine, trimmed
2 celery stalks, trimmed
4 large ripe tomatoes
1 tsp sunflower oil
2 shallots, peeled and
  finely chopped
1½ tsp tomato purée
25 g/1 oz green pitted olives
25 g/1 oz black pitted olives
salt and freshly ground black pepper
1 tbsp white wine vinegar
2 tsp caster sugar
1 tbsp freshly chopped basil,
  to garnish
mixed salad leaves, to serve

FOOD FACT

It has been suggested, that foods which are purple in colour, such as aubergines, have particularly powerful antioxidants, which help the body to protect itself from disease and strengthen the organs.

1 Preheat the oven to 200°C/400°F/Gas Mark 6. Cut the aubergine into small cubes and place on an oiled baking tray.

2 Cover the tray with tinfoil and bake in the preheated oven for 15–20 minutes until soft. Reserve, to allow the aubergine to cool.

3 Place the celery and tomatoes in a large bowl and cover with boiling water.

4 Remove the tomatoes from the bowl when their skins begin to peel away. Remove the skins then, deseed and chop the flesh into small pieces.

5 Remove the celery from the bowl of water, finely chop and reserve.

6 Pour the vegetable oil into a non-stick saucepan, add the chopped shallots and fry gently for 2–3 minutes until soft. Add the celery, tomatoes, tomato purée and olives. Season to taste with salt and pepper.

7 Simmer gently for 3–4 minutes. Add the vinegar, sugar and cooled aubergine to the pan and heat gently for 2–3 minutes until all the ingredients are well blended. Reserve to allow the aubergine mixture to cool. When cool, garnish with the chopped basil and serve cold with salad leaves.

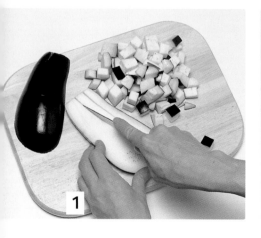

1

5

6

Carrot, Celeriac & Sesame Seed Salad

INGREDIENTS

Serves 6

225 g/8 oz celeriac
225 g/8 oz carrots, peeled
50 g/2 oz seedless raisins
2 tbsp sesame seeds
freshly chopped parsley, to garnish

Lemon & chilli dressing:

grated rind of 1 lemon
4 tbsp lemon juice
2 tbsp sunflower oil
2 tbsp clear honey
1 red bird's eye chilli, deseeded and
  finely chopped
salt and freshly ground black pepper

1 Slice the celeriac into thin matchsticks. Place in a small saucepan of boiling salted water and boil for 2 minutes.

2 Drain and rinse the celeriac in cold water and place in a mixing bowl.

3 Finely grate the carrot. Add the carrot and the raisins to the celeriac in the bowl.

4 Place the sesame seeds under a hot grill or dry-fry in a frying pan for 1–2 minutes until golden brown, then leave to cool.

5 Make the dressing by whisking together the lemon rind, lemon juice, oil, honey, chilli and seasoning or by shaking thoroughly in a screw-topped jar.

6 Pour 2 tablespoons of the dressing over the salad and toss well. Turn into a serving dish and sprinkle over the toasted sesame seeds and chopped parsley. Serve the remaining dressing separately.

FOOD FACT

Celeriac is a root vegetable that is similar in taste to fennel, but with a texture closer to parsnip. This versatile vegetable has a creamy taste and is also delicious in soups and gratins.

1

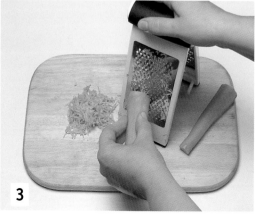

3

4

Crispy Baked Potatoes with Serrano Ham

INGREDIENTS

Serves 4

4 large baking potatoes
4 tsp half-fat crème fraîche
salt and freshly ground black pepper
50 g/2 oz lean serrano ham or
 prosciutto, with fat removed
50 g/2 oz cooked baby broad beans
50 g/2 oz cooked carrots, diced
50 g/2 oz cooked peas
50 g/2 oz low-fat hard cheese such as
 Edam or Cheddar, grated
fresh green salad, to serve

1 Preheat the oven to 200°C/400°F/Gas Mark 6. Scrub the potatoes dry. Prick with a fork and place on a baking sheet. Cook for 1–1½ hours or until tender when squeezed. (Use oven gloves or a kitchen towel to pick up the potatoes as they will be very hot.)

2 Cut the potatoes in half horizontally and scoop out all the flesh into a bowl.

3 Spoon the crème fraîche into the bowl and mix thoroughly with the potatoes. Season to taste with a little salt and pepper.

4 Cut the ham into strips and carefully stir into the potato mixture with the broad beans, carrots and peas.

5 Pile the mixture back into the 8 potato shells and sprinkle a little grated cheese on the top.

6 Place under a hot grill and cook until golden and heated through. Serve immediately with a fresh green salad.

FOOD FACT

Produced in Spain, serrano ham has a succulent sweet taste and is traditionally carved along the grain. The nearest substitute is prosciutto. Serrano ham has a chewy texture and is often served in thin slices on bread.

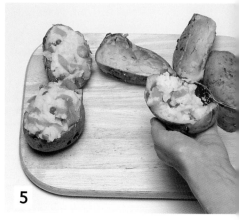

Orange Freeze

INGREDIENTS

Serves 4

4 large oranges
about 300 ml/½ pint low-fat vanilla
  ice cream
225 g/8 oz raspberries
75 g/3 oz icing sugar, sifted
redcurrant sprigs, to decorate

TASTY TIP

The fresh citrus in this dish works to clear the palate. The acidity combines well with the creaminess of the ice cream. Orange is very good with mango, so why not experiment by adding the flesh of a small ripe mango in step 4 for a more fragrant dessert? Lemons would also work well in this recipe.

1 Set the freezer to rapid freeze. Using a sharp knife carefully cut the lid off each orange.

2 Scoop out the flesh from the orange, discarding any pips and thick pith.

3 Place the shells and lids in the freezer and chop any remaining orange flesh.

4 Whisk together the orange juice, orange flesh and vanilla ice cream, until well blended.

5 Cover and freeze, for about 2 hours, occasionally breaking up the ice crystals with a fork or a whisk. Stir the mixture from around the edge of the container into the centre, then level and return to the freezer. Do this 2–3 times then leave until almost frozen solid.

6 Place a large scoop of the ice cream mixture into the frozen shells. Add another scoop on top, so that there is plenty outside of the orange shell and return to the freezer for 1 hour.

7 Arrange the lids on top and freeze for a further 2 hours, until the filled orange shell is completely frozen solid.

8 Meanwhile, using a nylon sieve press the raspberries into a bowl using the back of a wooden spoon and mix together with the icing sugar. Spoon the raspberry coulis on to 4 serving plates and place an orange at the centre of each. Dust with icing sugar and serve decorated with the redcurrants. Remember to return the freezer to its normal setting.

2

5

8

Chocolate Mousse

INGREDIENTS

Serves 6

175 g/6 oz milk or plain
   chocolate orange
535 g carton half-fat
   ready-made custard
450 ml/³/₄ pint half-fat
   double cream
12 Cape gooseberries, to decorate
sweet reduced-fat biscuits, to serve

FOOD FACT

Cape gooseberries are also known as Physallis and can be found in most major supermarkets. They have a sweet flavour with a slight acidity. Similar in taste to yogurt.

HELPFUL HINT

Have fun with the presentation of this dish. Why not serve in large cappuccino cups and lightly dust with some cocoa powder or icing sugar. Serve plenty of the gooseberries for guests to dip into the chocolate mousse.

1 Break the chocolate into segments and place in a bowl set over a saucepan of simmering water. Leave until melted, stirring occasionally. Remove the bowl in the pan from the heat and allow the melted chocolate to cool slightly.

2 Place the custard in a bowl and fold the melted chocolate into it using a metal spoon or rubber spatula. Stir well until completely combined.

3 Pour the cream into a small bowl and whip until the cream forms soft peaks.

4 Using a metal spoon or rubber spatula fold in most of the whipped cream into the chocolate mixture.

5 Spoon into six tall glasses and carefully top with the remaining cream.

6 Leave the desserts to chill in the refrigerator for at least 1 hour or preferably overnight.

7 Peel back the skins from the gooseberries to form petal shapes and use to decorate the chocolate desserts. Serve with sweet reduced-fat biscuits.

1

2

4

Creamy Puddings with Mixed Berry Compote

INGREDIENTS

Serves 6

300 ml/½ pint half-fat
   double cream
1 x 250 g carton ricotta cheese
50 g/2 oz caster sugar
125 g/4 oz white chocolate, broken
   into pieces
350 g/12 oz mixed summer fruits
   such as strawberries, blueberries
   and raspberries
2 tbsp Cointreau

TASTY TIP

Why not try mulled fruit compote with this recipe? Poach 4–6 dark plums quartered and 4 dessert pears sliced into thick wedges in 150 ml/¼ pint of red wine. Add 1 mulled wine sachet, 1–2 tablespoons of sugar and 2 cinnamon sticks. Simmer until reduced by half and the fruit has softened. Remove from the heat and discard the mulled wine sachet. Allow to cool before spooning over the pudding. Decorate with strips of orange rind.

1 Set the freezer to rapid freeze. Whip the cream until soft peaks form. Fold in the ricotta cheese and half the sugar.

2 Place the chocolate in a bowl set over a saucepan of simmering water. Stir until melted.

3 Remove from the heat and leave to cool, stirring occasionally. Stir into the cheese mixture until well blended.

4 Spoon the mixture into 6 individual pudding moulds and level the surface of each pudding with the back of a spoon. Place in the freezer and freeze for 4 hours.

5 Place the fruits and the remaining sugar in a pan and heat gently, stirring occasionally until the sugar has dissolved and the juices are just beginning to run. Stir in the Cointreau to taste.

6 Dip the pudding moulds in hot water for 30 seconds and invert on to 6 serving plates. Spoon the fruit compote over the puddings and serve immediately. Remember to return the freezer to its normal setting.

Rice Pudding

INGREDIENTS

Serves 4

60 g/2½ oz pudding rice
50 g/2 oz granulated sugar
410 g can light evaporated milk
300 ml/½ pint semi-
  skimmed milk
pinch of freshly grated nutmeg
25 g/1 oz half-fat butter
reduced sugar jam, to decorate

TASTY TIP

Traditionally, rice pudding was cooked alongside the Sunday roast which, after many hours in the oven, came out rich and creamy. The main trick to achieving traditional creamy rice pudding is not using cream and full-fat milk, but instead long, slow cooking on a low temperature. Try adding a few sultanas and lemon peel, or a few roughly crushed cardamom pods for an alternative flavour. It is also delicious dusted with a little ground cinnamon.

1 Preheat the oven to 150°C/300°F/Gas Mark 2. Lightly oil a large ovenproof dish.

2 Sprinkle the rice and the sugar into the dish and mix.

3 Bring the evaporated milk and milk to the boil in a small pan, stirring occasionally.

4 Stir the milks into the rice and mix well until the rice is coated thoroughly.

5 Sprinkle over the nutmeg, cover with tinfoil and bake in the preheated oven for 30 minutes.

6 Remove the pudding from the oven and stir well, breaking up any lumps.

7 Cover with the same tinfoil. Bake in the preheated oven for a further 30 minutes. Remove from the oven and stir well again.

8 Dot the pudding with butter and bake for a further 45–60 minutes, until the rice is tender and the skin is browned.

9 Divide the pudding into 4 individual serving bowls. Top with a large spoonful of the jam and serve immediately.

2

4

6

Lemon Surprise

INGREDIENTS

Serves 4

75 g /3 oz half-fat margarine
175 g/6 oz caster sugar
3 medium eggs, separated
75 g/3 oz self-raising flour
450 ml/³/₄ pint semi-
  skimmed milk
juice of 2 lemons
juice of 1 orange
2 tsp icing sugar
lemon twists, to decorate
sliced strawberries, to serve

FOOD FACT

This recipe uses a bain-marie, (when the dish is placed in a tin as in step 6) which enables the pudding to cook slower. This is necessary as half-fat margarine does not respond well if baked at high temperatures.

1 Preheat the oven to 190°C/375°F/Gas Mark 5. Lightly oil a deep ovenproof dish.

2 Beat together the margarine and sugar until pale and fluffy.

3 Add the egg yolks, one at a time, with 1 tablespoon of the flour and beat well after each addition. Once added, stir in the remaining flour.

4 Stir in the milk, 4 tablespoons of the lemon juice and 3 tablespoons of the orange juice.

5 Whisk the egg whites until stiff and fold into the pudding mixture with a metal spoon or rubber spatula until well combined. Pour into the prepared dish.

6 Stand the dish in a roasting tin and pour in just enough boiling water to come halfway up the sides of the dish.

7 Bake in the preheated oven for 45 minutes, until well risen and spongy to the touch.

8 Remove the pudding from the oven and sprinkle with the icing sugar. Decorate with the lemon twists and serve immediately with the strawberries.

3

5

6

Orange Curd & Plum Puddings

INGREDIENTS

Serves 4

700 g/1½ lb plums, stoned
  and quartered
2 tbsp light brown sugar
grated rind of ½ lemon
25 g/1 oz butter, melted
1 tbsp olive oil
6 sheets filo pastry
½ x 411 g jar luxury orange curd
50 g/2 oz sultanas
icing sugar, to decorate
half-fat thick set Greek yogurt,
  to serve

1 Preheat the oven to 200°C/400° F/Gas Mark 6. Lightly oil a 20.5 cm/8 inch round cake tin. Cook the plums with 2 tablespoons of the light brown sugar for 8–10 minutes to soften them, remove from the heat and reserve.

2 Mix together the lemon rind, butter and oil. Lay a sheet of pastry in the prepared cake tin and brush with the lemon rind mixture.

3 Cut the sheets of filo pastry in half and then place one half sheet in the cake tin and brush again.

4 Top with the remaining halved sheets of pastry brushing each time with the lemon rind mixture. Fold each sheet in half lengthways to line the sides of the tin to make a filo case.

5 Mix together the plums, orange curd and sultanas and spoon into the pastry case.

6 Draw the pastry edges up over the filling to enclose. Brush the remaining sheets of filo pastry with the lemon rind mixture and cut into thick strips.

7 Scrunch each strip of pastry and arrange on top of the pie. Bake in the preheated oven for 25 minutes, until golden. Sprinkle with icing sugar and serve with the Greek yogurt.

HELPFUL HINT

Filo pastry dries out very quickly. Keep wrapped when not using.

2

5

7

Coffee & Peach Creams

INGREDIENTS

Serves 4

4 peaches
50 g/2 oz caster sugar
2 tbsp coffee essence
200 g carton half-fat Greek
  set yogurt
300 g carton half-fat
  ready-made custard

To decorate:
peach slices
sprigs of mint
low-fat crème fraîche

1 Cut the peaches in half and remove the stones. Place the peaches in a large bowl, cover with boiling water and leave for 2–3 minutes.

2 Drain the peaches, then carefully remove the skin. Using a sharp knife, halve the peaches.

3 Place the caster sugar in a saucepan and add 50 ml/2 fl oz water.

4 Bring the sugar mixture to the boil, stirring occasionally, until the sugar has dissolved. Boil rapidly for about 2 minutes.

5 Add the peaches and coffee essence to the pan. Remove from the heat and allow the peach mixture to cool.

6 Meanwhile mix together the Greek yogurt and custard until well combined.

7 Divide the peaches between the 4 glass dishes.

8 Spoon over the custard mixture then top with the remaining peach mixture.

9 Chill for 30 minutes and then serve, decorated with peach slices, mint sprigs and a little crème fraîche.

FOOD FACT

It is generally believed that peaches originated from China. There are over 2,000 varieties grown throughout the world.

2

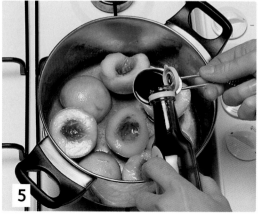

5

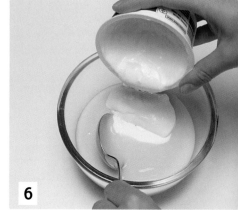

6

Sweet–stewed Dried Fruits

INGREDIENTS

Serves 4

500 g/1 lb 2 oz packet mixed dried
  fruit salad
450 ml/³/₄ pint apple juice
2 tbsp clear honey
2 tbsp brandy
1 lemon
1 orange

To decorate:

half-fat crème fraîche
fine strips of pared orange rind

TASTY TIP

As a dessert, this dish is particularly good when served with cold rice pudding. However, these stewed fruits can also be very nice for breakfast. Simply pour some unsweetened muesli into the bottom of a bowl, top with the stewed fruits and perhaps some low-fat natural yogurt and serve.

1 Place the fruits, apple juice, clear honey and brandy in a small saucepan.

2 Using a small, sharp knife or a zester, carefully remove the zest from the lemon and orange and place in the pan.

3 Squeeze the juice from the lemon and oranges and add to the pan.

4 Bring the fruit mixture to the boil and simmer for about 1 minute. Remove the pan from the heat and allow the mixture to cool completely.

5 Transfer the mixture to a large bowl, cover with clingfilm and chill in the refrigerator overnight to allow the flavours to blend.

6 Spoon the stewed fruit in 4 shallow dessert dishes. Decorate with a large spoonful of half-fat crème fraîche and a few strips of the pared orange rind and serve.

Chocolate Brandy Dream

INGREDIENTS

Serves 4

175 g/6 oz low-fat chocolate, broken
  into pieces
300 ml/½ pint whipping cream
2 tbsp brandy
1 tbsp coffee essence
1 medium egg white

To decorate:

raspberries
blueberries
mint leaves
cocoa powder

FOOD FACT

Careful blending is the key to recipe success in this dish, as it relies on the air beaten into both the cream and the egg whites to support the fairly heavy chocolate mixture. Take particular care when folding in the egg whites – you may find that folding just a tablespoon of the egg whites into the cream mixture may loosen the mixture and make it easier to then fold into the rest of the egg whites.

1 Place the pieces of chocolate into a heat-proof bowl placed over a saucepan of gently simmering water and leave to slowly melt, stirring occasionally.

2 Carefully remove the pan and the bowl from the heat and reserve to allow the chocolate to cool.

3 Pour the cream into a small bowl, whip until soft peaks form, then reserve.

4 Gently stir the brandy and coffee essence into the chocolate. Mix together gently until blended, then fold in the whipped cream with a metal spoon or rubber spatula.

5 Briskly whisk the egg white in a small bowl until stiff, then fold into the chocolate mixture with a metal spoon or rubber spatula.

6 Mix the chocolate mixture gently, taking care not to remove the air already whisked into the egg white.

7 Spoon into 4 tall glasses and chill for at least 2 hours. Decorate with raspberries, blueberries and mint leaves. Dust with cocoa powder and serve.

1

3

5

Autumn Fruit Layer

INGREDIENTS

Serves 4

450 g/1 lb Bramley cooking apples
225 g/8 oz blackberries
50 g/2 oz soft brown sugar
juice of 1 lemon
50 g/2 oz low-fat spread
200 g/7 oz breadcrumbs
225 g/8 oz honey-coated
  nut mix, chopped
redcurrants and mint leaves,
  to decorate
half-fat whipped cream or reduced-fat
  ice cream, to serve

TASTY TIP

Any autumn fruit can be used in this recipe. Add pear to this recipe to make an apple and pear fruit layer or use some plums if preferred. For a more textured pudding, reduce the amount of breadcrumbs used to 150 g/5 oz and add 50 g/2 oz of rolled oats in step 5.

1 Peel, core and slice the cooking apples and place in a saucepan with the blackberries, sugar and lemon juice.

2 Cover the fruit mixture and simmer, stirring occasionally for about 15 minutes or until the apples and blackberries have formed into a thick purée.

3 Remove the pan from the heat and allow to cool.

4 Melt the low-fat spread in a frying pan and cook the breadcrumbs for 5–10 minutes, stirring occasionally until golden and crisp.

5 Remove the pan from the heat and stir in the nuts. Allow to cool.

6 Alternately layer the fruit purée and breadcrumbs into 4 tall glasses.

7 Store the desserts in the refrigerator to chill and remove when ready to serve.

8 Decorate with redcurrants and mint leaves and serve with half-fat whipped cream or a reduced-fat vanilla or raspberry ice cream.

1

4

6

Oaty Fruit Puddings

INGREDIENTS

Serves 4

125 g/4 oz rolled oats
50 g/2 oz low-fat spread, melted
2 tbsp chopped almonds
1 tbsp clear honey
pinch of ground cinnamon
2 pears, peeled, cored and
    finely chopped
1 tbsp marmalade
orange zest, to decorate
low-fat custard or fruit-flavoured
    low-fat yogurt, to serve

1 Preheat the oven to 200°C/400°F/Gas Mark 6. Lightly oil and line the bases of 4 individual pudding bowls or muffin tins with a small circle of greaseproof paper.

2 Mix together the oats, low-fat spread, nuts, honey and cinnamon in a small bowl.

3 Using a spoon, spread two thirds of the oaty mixture over the base and around the sides of the pudding bowls or muffin tins.

4 Toss together the pears and marmalade and spoon into the oaty cases.

5 Scatter over the remaining oaty mixture to cover the pears and marmalade.

6 Bake in the preheated oven for 15–20 minutes, until cooked and the tops of the puddings are golden and crisp.

7 Leave for 5 minutes before removing the pudding bowls or the muffin tins. Decorate with orange zest and serve hot with low-fat custard or low-fat fruit-flavoured yogurt.

TASTY TIP

Liqueur custard is superb with steamed and baked puddings. Add 2–3 tablespoons of either Cointreau or a liqueur of your choice to the custard, together with 1 teaspoon of vanilla essence. Taste the custard and add more alcohol if desired.

1

3

4

Fruit Salad

INGREDIENTS

Serves 4

125 g/4 oz caster sugar
3 oranges
700 g/1½ lb lychees, peeled
  and stoned
1 small mango
1 small pineapple
1 papaya
4 pieces stem ginger in syrup
4 tbsp stem ginger syrup
125 g/4 oz Cape gooseberries
125 g/4 oz strawberries, hulled
½ tsp almond essence

To decorate:

lime zest
mint leaves

FOOD FACT

A fruit salad is the perfect end to a good meal because it refreshes the palate and is also packed full of vitamins.

1 Place the sugar and 300 ml/½ pint of water in a small pan and heat, gently stirring until the sugar has dissolved. Bring to the boil and simmer for 2 minutes. Once a syrup has formed, remove from the heat and allow to cool.

2 Using a sharp knife, cut away the skin from the oranges, then slice thickly. Cut each slice in half and place in a serving dish with the syrup and lychees.

3 Peel the mango, then cut into thick slices around each side of the stone. Discard the stone and cut the slices into bite-sized pieces and add to the syrup.

4 Using a sharp knife again, carefully cut away the skin from the pineapple.

5 Remove the central core using the knife or an apple corer, then cut the pineapple into segments and add to the syrup.

6 Peel the papaya, then cut in half and remove the seeds. Cut the flesh into chunks, slice the ginger into matchsticks and add with the ginger syrup to the fruit in the syrup.

7 Prepare the Cape gooseberries, by removing the thin, papery skins and rinsing lightly.

8 Halve the strawberries, add to the fruit with the almond essence and chill for 30 minutes. Scatter with mint leaves and lime zest to decorate and serve.

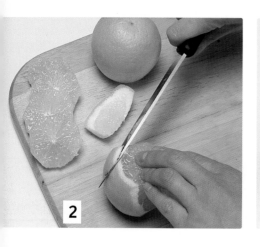

2

3

4

Summer Pavlova

INGREDIENTS

Serves 6-8

4 medium egg whites
225 g/8 oz caster sugar
1 tsp vanilla essence
2 tsp white wine vinegar
1½ tsp cornflour
300 ml/½ pint half-fat
   Greek-set yogurt
2 tbsp honey
225 g/8 oz strawberries, hulled
125 g/4 oz raspberries
125 g/4 oz blueberries
4 kiwis, peeled and sliced
icing sugar, to decorate

1 Preheat the oven to 150°C/300°F/Gas Mark 2. Line a baking sheet with a sheet of greaseproof or baking parchment paper.

2 Place the egg whites in a clean grease-free bowl and whisk until very stiff.

3 Whisk in half the sugar, vanilla essence, vinegar and cornflour, continue whisking until stiff.

4 Gradually, whisk in the remaining sugar, a teaspoonful at a time until very stiff and glossy.

5 Using a large spoon, arrange spoonfuls of the meringue in a circle on the greaseproof paper or baking parchment paper.

6 Bake in the preheated oven for 1 hour until crisp and dry. Turn the oven off and leave the meringue in the oven to cool completely.

7 Remove the meringue from the baking sheet and peel away the parchment paper. Mix together the yogurt and honey. Place the pavlova on a serving plate and spoon the yogurt into the centre.

8 Scatter over the strawberries, raspberries, blueberries and kiwis. Dust with the icing sugar and serve.

HELPFUL HINT

Always remember to double check that the bowl being used to whisk egg whites is completely clean, as you will find that any grease will prevent the egg whites from rising into the stiff consistency necessary for this recipe.

3

5

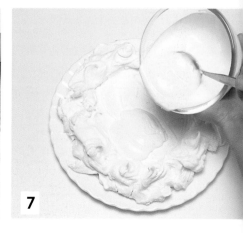

7

Poached Pears

INGREDIENTS

Serves 4

2 small cinnamon sticks
125 g/4 oz caster sugar
300 ml/½ pint red wine
150 ml/¼ pint water
thinly pared rind and juice of
  1 small orange
4 firm pears
orange slices, to decorate
frozen vanilla yogurt, or low-fat ice
  cream, to serve

TASTY TIP

Poached pears are delicious served with a little half-fat crème fraîche and sprinkled with toasted almonds. To toast almonds, simply warm the grill and place whole, blanched almonds or flaked almonds on to a piece of tinfoil. Place under the grill and toast lightly on both sides for 1–2 minutes until golden. Remove and cool, chop if liked.

1 Place the cinnamon sticks on the work surface and with a rolling pin, slowly roll down the side of the cinnamon stick to bruise. Place in a large heavy-based saucepan.

2 Add the sugar, wine, water, pared orange rind and juice to the pan and bring slowly to the boil, stirring occasionally, until the sugar is dissolved.

3 Meanwhile peel the pears, leaving the stalks on.

4 Cut out the cores from the bottom of the pears and level them so that they stand upright.

5 Stand the pears in the syrup, cover the pan and simmer for 20 minutes or until tender.

6 Remove the pan from the heat and leave the pears to cool in the syrup, turning occasionally.

7 Arrange the pears on serving plates and spoon over the syrup. Decorate with the orange slices and serve with the yogurt or low-fat ice cream and any remaining juices.

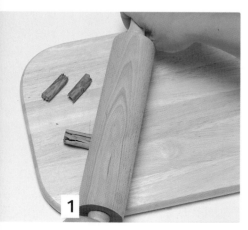

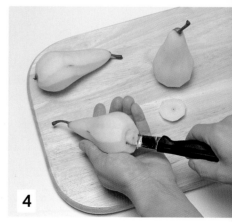

Grape & Almond Layer

INGREDIENTS

Serves 4

300 ml/½ pint low-fat
   fromage frais
300 ml/½ pint half-fat
   Greek-set yogurt
3 tbsp icing sugar, sifted
2 tbsp crème de cassis
450 g/1 lb red grapes
175 g/6 oz Amaretti biscuits
2 ripe passion fruit

To decorate:

icing sugar
extra grapes, optional

1. Mix together the fromage frais and yogurt in a bowl and lightly fold in the sifted icing sugar and crème de cassis with a large metal spoon or rubber spatula until lightly blended.

2. Using a small knife, remove the seeds from the grapes if necessary. Rinse lightly and pat dry on absorbent kitchen paper.

3. Place the deseeded grapes in a bowl and stir in any juice from the grapes from deseeding.

4. Place the Amaretti biscuits in a polythene bag and crush roughly with a rolling pin. (Alternatively, use a food processor.)

5. Cut the passion fruit in half, scoop out the seeds with a teaspoon and reserve.

6. Divide the yogurt mixture between 4 tall glasses, then layer alternately with grapes, crushed biscuits and most of the passion fruit seeds. Top with the yogurt mixture and the remaining passion fruit seeds. Chill for 1 hour and decorate with extra grapes. Lightly dust with icing sugar and serve.

FOOD FACT

Passion fruits are native to Brazil. They are purple in colour and are about the size of an egg. Look for fruits that are wrinkled, not smooth. When wrinkled they are ripe and at their best.

1

2

5

Summer Pudding

INGREDIENTS

Serves 4

450 g/1 lb redcurrants
125 g/4 oz caster sugar
350 g/12 oz strawberries, hulled
 and halved
125 g/4 oz raspberries
2 tbsp Grand Marnier or Cointreau
8–10 medium slices white bread,
 crusts removed
mint sprigs, to decorate
low-fat Greek-set yogurt or low-fat
 fromage frais, to serve

TASTY TIP

This really is a summer pudding, using plump, juicy berries that are bursting with flavour. Why not try an autumn version using seasonal fruit such as blackberries, plums and flavoursome apples? Place in just a few tablespoons of water, together with 50 g/2 oz of caster sugar and heat gently as in step 1.

1 Place the redcurrants, sugar and 1 tablespoon of water in a large saucepan. Heat gently until the sugar has just dissolved and the juices have just begun to run.

2 Remove the saucepan from the heat and stir in the strawberries, raspberries and the Grand Marnier or Cointreau.

3 Line the base and sides of a 1.1 litre/2 pint pudding basin with two thirds of the bread, making sure that the slices overlap each other slightly.

4 Spoon the fruit with their juices into the bread-lined pudding basin, then top with the remaining bread slices.

5 Place a small plate on top of the pudding inside the pudding basin. Ensure the plate fits tightly, then weigh down with a clean can or some weights and chill in the refrigerator overnight.

6 When ready to serve, remove the weights and plate. Carefully loosen round the sides of the basin with a round-bladed knife. Invert the pudding on to a serving plate, decorate with the mint sprigs and serve with the yogurt or fromage frais.

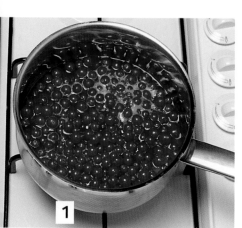

1

3

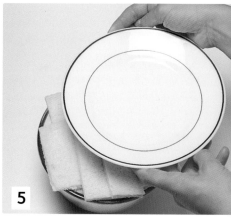

5

Caramelised Oranges in an Iced Bowl

INGREDIENTS

Serves 4

8 medium-sized oranges
225 g/8 oz caster sugar
4 tbsp Grand Marnier or Cointreau

For the ice bowl:

about 36 ice cubes
fresh flowers and fruits

1 Set freezer to rapid freeze. Place a few ice cubes in the base of a 1.7 litre/3 pint freezable glass bowl. Place a 900 ml/1½ pint glass bowl on top of the ice cubes. Arrange the flower heads and fruits in between the 2 bowls, wedging in position with the ice cubes.

2 Weigh down the smaller bowl with some heavy weights, then carefully pour cold water between the 2 bowls making sure that the flowers and the fruit are covered. Freeze for at least 6 hours or until the ice is frozen solid.

3 When ready to use, remove the weights and using a hot damp cloth rub the inside of the smaller bowl with the cloth until it loosens sufficiently for you to remove the bowl. Place the larger bowl in the sink or washing-up bowl, half filled with very hot water. Leave for about 30 seconds or until the ice loosens. Take care not to leave the bowl in the water for too long otherwise the ice will melt. Remove the bowl and leave in the refrigerator. Return the freezer to its normal setting.

4 Thinly pare the rind from 2 oranges and then cut into julienne strips. Using a sharp knife cut away the rind and pith from all the oranges, holding over a bowl to catch the juices. Slice the oranges, discarding any pips and reform each orange back to its original shape. Secure with cocktail sticks, then place in a bowl.

5 Heat 300 ml/½ pint water, orange rind and sugar together in a pan. Stir the sugar until dissolved. Bring to the boil. Boil for 15 minutes, until it is a caramel colour. Remove pan from heat.

6 Stir in the liqueur, pour over the oranges. Allow to cool. Chill for 3 hours, turning the oranges occasionally. Spoon into the ice bowl and serve.

HELPFUL HINT

This iced bowl can hold any dessert. Why not fill with flavoured ice creams?

1

2

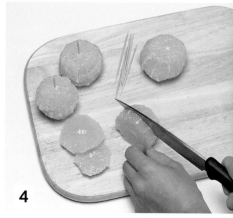

4

Raspberry Sorbet Crush

INGREDIENTS

Serves 4

225 g/8 oz raspberries,
 thawed if frozen
grated rind and juice of 1 lime
300 ml/½ pint orange juice
225 g/8 oz caster sugar
2 medium egg whites

1 Set the freezer to rapid freeze. If using fresh raspberries pick over and lightly rinse.

2 Place the raspberries in a dish and, using a masher, mash to a chunky purée.

3 Place the lime rind and juice, orange juice and half the caster sugar in a large heavy-based saucepan.

4 Heat gently stirring frequently until the sugar is dissolved. Bring to the boil and boil rapidly for about 5 minutes.

5 Remove the pan from the heat and pour carefully into a freezable container.

6 Leave to cool, then place in the freezer and freeze for 2 hours, stirring occasionally to break up the ice crystals.

7 Fold the ice mixture into the raspberry purée with a metal spoon and freeze for a further 2 hours, stirring occasionally.

8 Whisk the egg whites until stiff. Then gradually whisk in the remaining caster sugar a tablespoon at a time until the egg white mixture is stiff and glossy.

9 Fold into the raspberry sorbet with a metal spoon and freeze for 1 hour. Spoon into tall glasses and serve immediately. Remember to return the freezer to its normal setting.

FOOD FACT

This recipe contains raw egg and should not be given to babies, young children, pregnant women, the sick, the elderly and those suffering from a recurring illness.

2

7

9

Raspberry Soufflé

INGREDIENTS

Serves 4

125 g/4 oz redcurrants
50 g/2 oz caster sugar
1 sachet (3 tsp) powdered gelatine
3 medium eggs, separated
300 g/½ pint half-fat Greek yogurt
450 g/1 lb raspberries,
  thawed if frozen

To decorate:

mint sprigs
extra fruits

HELPFUL HINT

Soufflés rely on air, so it is important that the egg whites in this recipe are beaten until very stiff in order to support the other mixture.

1. Wrap a band of double thickness greaseproof paper around four ramekin dishes, making sure that 5 cm/2 inches of the paper stays above the top of each dish. Secure the paper to the dish with an elastic band or Sellotape.

2. Place the redcurrants and 1 tablespoon of the sugar in a small saucepan. Cook for 5 minutes until softened. Remove from the heat, sieve and reserve.

3. Place 3 tablespoons of water in a small bowl and sprinkle over the gelatine. Allow to stand for 5 minutes until spongy. Place the bowl over a pan of simmering water and leave until dissolved. Remove and allow to cool.

4. Beat together the remaining sugar and egg yolks until pale thick and creamy, then fold in the yogurt with a metal spoon or rubber spatula until well blended.

5. Sieve the raspberries and fold into the yogurt mixture with the gelatine. Whisk the egg whites until stiff and fold into the yogurt mixture. Pour into the prepared dishes and chill in the refrigerator for 2 hours until firm.

6. Remove the paper from the dishes and spread the redcurrant purée over the top of the soufflés. Decorate with mint sprigs and extra fruits and serve.

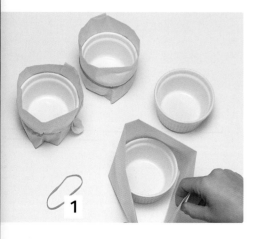

1

3

5

Fruity Roulade

INGREDIENTS

Serves 4

For the sponge:

3 medium eggs
75 g/3 oz caster sugar
75 g/3 oz plain flour, sieved
1–2 tbsp caster sugar for sprinkling

For the filling:

125 g/4 oz Quark
125 g/4 oz half-fat Greek yogurt
25 g/1 oz caster sugar
1 tbsp orange liqueur (optional)
grated rind of 1 orange
125 g/4 oz strawberries, hulled and
  cut into quarters

To decorate:

strawberries
sifted icing sugar

FOOD FACT

Quark is a soft unripened cheese with the flavour and texture of soured cream. It comes in 2 varieties, low fat and non-fat. Quark can be used as a sour cream substitute to top baked potatoes, or in dips and cheesecakes.

1 Preheat the oven to 220°C/425°F/Gas Mark 7. Lightly oil and line a 33 x 23 cm/13 x 9 inch Swiss roll tin with greaseproof or baking parchment paper.

2 Using an electric whisk, whisk the eggs and sugar until the mixture is double in volume and leaves a trail across the top.

3 Fold in the flour with a metal spoon or rubber spatula. Pour into the prepared tin and bake in the preheated oven for 10–12 minutes, until well risen and golden.

4 Place a whole sheet of greaseproof or baking parchment paper out on a flat work surface and sprinkle evenly with caster sugar.

5 Turn the cooked sponge out on to the paper, discard the paper, trim the sponge and roll up encasing the paper inside. Reserve until cool.

6 To make the filling, mix together the Quark, yogurt, caster sugar, liqueur (if using) and orange rind. Unroll the roulade and spread over the mixture. Scatter over the strawberries and roll up.

7 Decorate the roulade with the strawberries. Dust with the icing sugar and serve.

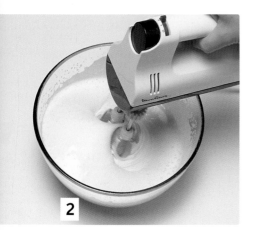

2

5

6

Index